Radical Christianity
and Its Sources

Radical Christianity and Its Sources

by

JOHN CHARLES COOPER

THE WESTMINSTER PRESS
Philadelphia

Copyright © MCMLXVIII The Westminster Press

Scripture quotations from the Revised Standard Version of the Bible are copyright, 1946 and 1952, by the Division of Christian Education of the National Council of Churches, and are used by permission.

LIBRARY OF CONGRESS CATALOG CARD No. 68–21411

Published by The Westminster Press®
Philadelphia, Pennsylvania

PRINTED IN THE UNITED STATES OF AMERICA

This book is dedicated to my parents,
Chauncey and Margaret Cooper, who are
examples of that ideal of human service
which should serve to reform the church

Preface

In a very real way the present-day mavericks of theology, the unsettled thinkers, the risk takers, the protesting voices that have been increasingly more prominent in America since 1961 are genuine children of the reforming spirit within Christendom. This book is thus a parallel to my earlier book, *The Roots of the Radical Theology* (The Westminster Press, 1967), which investigated the historical influences and forces that brought about the rise of the proclamation of the "death of God." In that book I directly charged that the intransigence of the "orthodox" church leaders and "institutional" theologians had made the several nineteenth- and twentieth-century attempts at a creative synthesis of faith and reason, church and world, fail, so that the more radical voices alone had a chance to give their answers to the questions raised by modern men who almost universally have experienced the loss of human self-transcendence. Because the church — as seen in its elected representatives and subsidized scholars — refused to take seriously the critiques and suggestions of Wilhelm Herrmann, Rudolf Bultmann, Albert Schweitzer, Paul Tillich, and other creative minds, preferring Karl Barth and Emil Brunner with their rejection of modern thought, the mantle of prophecy has now fallen on the most radical thinkers ever seen in Christianity.

This book is presented in the hope that it will carry through with the constructive, though radical, critique of the church

begun in *The Roots of the Radical Theology*. It will attempt a
twofold task: that of documenting the failure of the church to
be the church in the revolutionary days of the twentieth century and that of demonstrating the loyalty and rationality of
those critics who have so severely chastised church theology
and practice (and been so ignored) that they have been forced
to proclaim that "God is dead." My favorable appraisal (and
constant critique) of these "contrapuntal voices" in the first
book is the basis for this study. I have examined the works of
Thomas J. J. Altizer, William Hamilton, Richard L. Rubenstein,
and others like them and concluded that those who proclaim
the "death of God" do so out of loyalty to a living God, those
who denounce the present practice and traditional morals of
the church do so out of allegiance to the power of love, and
those who decry the "institutionalism" of the twentieth-century church do so out of a paradoxical faith in the spiritual
community that exists in the here and now, in spite of the pressures of a demonic church and a secular society against this
development. I want to underscore the genuine hope and love
of the radical critics who — consciously or unconsciously — react out of an outraged commitment to life and love, and who
have had the courage to wound the church in order to heal it.
This book is a study of the roots, the historical and social factors that make the new reformation necessary — and not of that
new reformation itself, since it does not yet appear what that
shall be. Thus, it only points (and hints) at the practical steps
that must be taken to bring a new reformation into being.

The author of these pages, who speaks so harshly of the
present-day institutional church, has no desire to defend himself against criticism for being such a vocal critic himself. On
the other hand, it may be of some value to the reader, and of
some support to his arguments, to record here that the author
is a minister of the Lutheran Church in America, a commis-
sioner of one of that church's agencies (Commission on Youth
Activities) and a frequent participant in church conferences

as well as a regular contributor of articles and studies to various church publications. This critique of the church, then, is not made from outside the church but from within. In the author's case, as well as in the case of some of the radical critics quoted within this book, criticism grows out of loyalty and interest, not out of rejection.

J. C. C.

Contents

Introduction

This is a book about the Christian church as it exists in the United States of America now. In a real sense, it is a phenomenology of the church — a description of the church and of the way it appears to those who feel as well as see. This is a picture of the church from the point of view of those who are concerned.

The picture drawn here is not a flattering one. Rather, this is intended to be an honest appraisal of that institution which lays claim to the centuries-old tradition that flows down to us from its sources in the life and work of Jesus who is called the Christ, the Anointed One of God: a life that was characterized by a brotherly love so genuine it healed those who accepted it and brought them to an integrity of life so unique that their lives turned the world of their day upside down. Unfortunately the picture presented here of the groups that still call themselves " Christ's men " reveals no such healing power or unique integrity. The contrast between the life of the namesake and the lives and, above all, the practices of the present-day Christian churchmen is stark. We look for " the man for others " and hear of him by the hearing of the ear — every Sunday from the pulpit — but we do not see this " man for others " with our eyes.

This book is, therefore, a call for a new reformation of the church — for a change in either profession or practice or both.

Like the simple peasants of the New Testament record, "we would see Jesus," for in our radical concern for the plight of our fellowmen, as well as in our radical concern for our own plight, we know that nothing less than a Christlike life is sufficient to aid us.

This book is harsh, because it is written out of disappointment. It may well be that some parts of this book will sound shrill in the ears of those who read it, because it has come forth from a quiet sense of outrage. This outrage is that modern, existential sense of traditional moral indignation which seems characteristic of the concerned individual living today in a land marred by interior and exterior injustice and made comfortable in its injustice by the platitudes of a large part of the clergy and church leaders of our era. If there is anger here, we hope it is akin to the holy anger of the prophets, for there is enough and too much of that unholy anger which splits men apart. May our harshness, our outrage, our anger prove a catharsis, and be taken as an acted parable of the real anger, the true disappointment, and the despairing outrage of the millions without the church, who, in Albert Camus's words waited for a great voice from Rome to cry out and denounce the evil that men do to one another in the modern world — and never heard it.

This book calls for a new reformation — a cleansing and a renewing of every part and every function of the church from the local congregation to the international assemblies of bishops, presidents, pastors, deacons, elders, and priests. The thesis of this book is that the church which does not serve all men of whatever status in life equally, in every area of their need, hope, and concern (physical, mental, moral, social, and material), is not worthy to be called a church but is a sham — a blasphemy upon the name of the Helping One; an insult to the sensitivity of every human being; and a blot that makes it all but impossible for men to come to an awareness of that Nameless One whose Biblical name is Love, and who — the radically aware and sensitive assure us — hears, heeds, feels, knows, suffers with us, and understands.

In the name then of the God of the future we here study the present by the aid of the past. If someone, somewhere feels the pull of that One who is beyond us and responds now, then the new reformation will have begun and this project will have accomplished its aim.

Chapter I
Is the Antithesis of Christianity "Christendom"?

For about a decade the Nietzschean slogan "God is dead" has been making the headlines in the American popular press in a manner that has delighted one minority group (the *avant-garde* thinkers), angered a slightly larger minority (our ultra-conservative religious people), and confused or missed altogether the majority of our secular-minded citizens. While there have always been philosophers and a few left-wing theological thinkers who have sifted through the body of Nietzsche's writings, finding there either scandalous or helpful insights according to their own presuppositions, it has been only recently that the meaning (whatever it may mean) of the madman's cry about the Divine Death has been given a serious hearing. The beginning date of the "modern" preoccupation with the claim that God is dead seems to be 1961. In that year Gabriel Vahanian [1] drew together several earlier articles in which he had explored the possibility that this age is the post-Christian era. Of course Vahanian had not originated the idea that this is the post-Christian era, an insight that was in general circulation and that owed something at least to Paul Tillich's argument, twenty-five years before, that we may have reached the end of the Protestant era. [2] The year 1961 also saw the appearance of *The New Essence of Christianity*, by William Hamilton, [3] and *Oriental Mysticism and Biblical Eschatology*, by Thomas J. J. Altizer. [4] Hamilton started the radical theological

ball rolling by writing about "belief in a time of the death of
God" and maintaining that the Biblical-Augustinian-Reformed
way of speaking about God simply leaves us cold, since it does
not deal adequately with the problem of radical evil.[5] However, Hamilton seemed safely on the side of the angels, since he
went no farther (at this point) than Paul Tillich and Martin
Buber, who also spoke of the experience of God's absence. In
1961, Hamilton was apparently still looking for God to return —
a position that he has since systematically denied in articles,
and that he proclaimed was a misunderstanding of his position
at the Conference on Radical Theology at Ann Arbor, Michigan, in October, 1966.[6] Thomas Altizer's work on mysticism
and eschatology also seemed singularly nonradical (compared
to his later work) as he concluded that while the Buddhist
mystic finds salvation in Nirvana or Nothingness, "the Christian must come to know the Nothing as the hither side of
God."[7]

However, in the years since 1961, a vague yet real movement has arisen within (and without) the Christian community
that has given a new sting to the adjective "radical." This
rather formless movement has been provoked by Altizer's and
Hamilton's ready access to the mediums of publicity and has
been given the journalistic name of "the 'death of God' theology." This "new theology" has now taken its place alongside the journalistically christened "new morality" trend
within the developing theological "new left" in America.

The Meaning of the Term "Radical" as Applied to Theology

Since every theological student recognizes that church history provides us with many examples of radical movements —
although we today may not recognize the precise degree of
their radicality in their own time — why the great disturbance
raised by the "new" (or "recent") radicals? To answer this
question properly demands a clear understanding of what the
term "radical" means when it modifies the noun "theology." A

radical movement in theology is one that cuts through the very heart of a system of thought and/or belief to the very foundations, "the roots," of that system. In the language of one Lutheran pastor, "radical thought really shoots a hole right through us." There isn't any way to be neutral about a radical critique, for if it is genuinely radical, it shoots holes in things that we at least thought we knew and thought we believed [8] before we were criticized.

Radical, therefore, means original, fundamental, reaching to the center or ultimate source, and a radical critique is thus thoroughgoing and extreme. If we reflect for a moment about theology and the church that produces such theological systems, we will realize that *only* radical critiques are worthwhile. Shallow criticisms of surface phenomena like church-related activities or liturgical practices mean little or nothing unless they grow out of a radical searching for Christianity's basic principles and beliefs. In the science of algebra a "radical expression" is a surd, a nonsense statement, but I would argue that in theology any expression of criticism that is not radical is actually a surd, that is, an irreducible lump of nonsense. Criticisms that neatly apologize for that which they supposedly are criticizing are nothing but illogical boulders that clutter the path to knowledge and hinder insight.

Perhaps the degree of power contained in the observation that criticism which does not cut to the bone, without mincing words, is useless is further illuminated by the following contrasting quotations:

The antithesis of Christianity is Christendom. (Kierkegaard.)

and

And upon this rock I will build my church; and the gates of hell shall not prevail against it. (Matt. 16:18, attributed to Jesus.)

The tension between the ideally conceived and the experientially actual is not new, nor is the oft-observed distinction

between the spirit and the flesh. Men have always looked upon
that which is historically exemplified in the church and judged
it as wanting compared with the church's own self-proclaimed
image of the ideal. In what sense, then, is the "death of God"
theology's attack new or more advanced than this common
complaint against the church?

Perhaps in the matter of the "death of God" theology we
have a case of quantity changing into quality. As I attempted
to point out in *The Roots of the Radical Theology*,[9] the new
form of radicalism is the outgrowth of the whole history of
negative religious thought in the West joined with the very religious critique of those who have opposed institutional religiosity from Søren Kierkegaard to Karl Barth. That which
makes the criticism of the new radicals so pertinent is the con-
junction in them of the negative or contrapuntal [10] tradition in
the West with the historically conditioned present experience
of the loss of the sense of human self-transcendence.

It was the contention of my first book that much of the
venom of radical thought both past and present has been
caused by the sheer intransigence of orthodox church leaders.
In other words, the excess conservatism of the church has
forced critics into positions much more extreme than they
ordinarily would have embraced. Useful illustrations of this
phenomenon are the experiences of the Catholic Church and
the Arians, and the treatment of those who called for reformation in the church in the centuries before the Protestant Reformation (John Hus, John Wycliffe, etc.).

The orthodox Catholic tradition was never the full story of
the philosophical and theological development of the West,
however. In fact, the orthodox tradition was hammered out by
a process of definition of the "correct" view of God, man, and
the world in a series of struggles with representatives of other
interpretations of the classical and Christian inheritance. Indeed, it is truthful to say that almost no element of the orthodox tradition of the West emerged without this process of test-

ing and refinement through opposition. In philosophy, the view of the universe as rational (one might call it the Apollonian tradition, as Nietzsche does [11]) was opposed from the beginnings of Western culture by the mythological, demonic view that saw the world as the product of divine (and irrational) forces. The term "Apollonian" was used by Nietzsche to denote the kind of world view that is orderly and rational. Apollo, the Greek deity — who oversaw the art of sculpture — was often contrasted with Dionysus, the wild, irrational god of music (and of drunkenness). Plato's belief in the immortality of the soul, which became a solid part of the orthodox Western tradition, had its opposition in Aristotle's philosophy— which, shorn of its "heresy" concerning the soul, itself became a large part of the Western tradition. In theology, the process of "indirect progress" by assertion and refutation is even clearer. Every one of the statements in the Nicene Creed and the Athanasian Creed was hammered out in this way: Arius versus Athanasius over the place of the person of Christ in the Godhead; Nestorius versus Cyril over the humanity of Christ; Eutyches versus the teachings of Cyril and Leo over the divinity of Christ. Without the "heretics" to keep them honest, the "orthodox" theologians would never have come to the fullest understanding of what they meant when they confessed, "Jesus is Lord."

It is this critical, antithetical tradition, often standing under the anathema of the church and the disdain of the academy, which I have designated the contrapuntal tradition. It forms "the other" that is essential to the self-identity of the orthodox tradition throughout the classical Greek, primitive Christian, "Dark," and Middle ages of Western culture.

Heresy

We ought to be clear about the meaning of "heresy" in this regard. The word "heresy" is derived from a Greek root meaning "choice." It is the election of another option, of another interpretation. At its strongest use, i.e., in its use to mean "false" doctrine, it means no more than "bad" theology. It does not have to mean "bad" religion, for religion and theology are not the same. Religion is one's effort to live by one's beliefs. Theology, on the other hand, is a systematic, rational presentation (and explanation) of what the religious community believes. Theology is the "science" of religion. One can "have religion" in the best sense and still be "heretical," i.e., give a different interpretation of what the community believes from what the official representatives of the community give. Unfortunately, this distinction works in reverse too. It is perfectly possible to present a "good" (i.e., accepted, orthodox) theology, and have little or no religion. In that case one looks upon the religion in question in the way that a philosopher may look upon a philosophical system that he does not personally accept. Or, equally unfortunately, one may pretend a concern for and loyalty to the religion and in actuality be a hypocrite. One's orthodoxy or lack of it is no guarantee that one is or is not "faithful." True religion has always been considered to be more than the acceptance of a catechism or creed.

It is my contention that however nonconformingly or disrespectfully Hamilton and Altizer have promulgated their views, they stand within the contrapuntal tradition that is vitally necessary to the theological health of the church. Although they may be shocking to some in their statements and may have used television and popular periodicals to present their critiques, they cannot be shunted aside, for in them the radical voice that keeps the church honest is speaking. Their willingness to recognize that the loss of the sense of self-transcendence is widespread within the church as well as without makes them, no matter how worthy or unworthy theologically they may be, the cutting edge of what Tillich called the Protestant principle. In them the prophetic spirit of the great critics of Western culture is working. The amusing and shocking way in which they speak is reminiscent of Erasmus' *The Praise of Folly*. Altizer and his followers (and there are many more young religion teachers and pastors who identify themselves with the "death of God" movement than is generally known) are describing for us experiences that we all share, not offering to us a private vision. They are authentic witnesses to our life situation as completely secularized men living in a "basically desacralized cosmos," even while we are members of the church. These radical younger theologians are thus still members of the theological circle, because they have the tradition of Western Christendom and the question about God as the object of their ultimate concern. They also display the courage to be, in spite of the sense of the meaninglessness of life so prevalent in Western culture today. Additionally, for each major radical — Altizer, Hamilton, and van Buren — Jesus is of paramount importance. Each is radically Christocentric in his thought, revealing the lineal continuity of this movement with the older Christocentric, socioethically-oriented liberalism. Even if the theologians of this "school" become known as "atheologians," "antitheologians," or Christian atheists, they are still, demonstrably, Christian.

The Provocation That Led to Radical Theology

What has provoked the rise of the "death of God" theology? Why have Altizer and Hamilton, who revere Tillich, moved to the left of Tillich's denunciation of popularly conceived personal theism to proclaim the death of God?

The generation before us passed through the experiences of demythologizing the gospel, hoping to recover its inner meaning. Our problem is that we not only reject the literalism of mythology (which has been the position of theologians for a long time) but we no longer believe in the meaning of the broken myths. Our generation has finally seen that it has lost the hope of human self-transcendence. Tillich was able to provide a corrective for Bultmann for the last generation, but he is not enough for ours. Not even a broken myth demythologized and explained in terms of Jung and depth psychology will suffice. Our generation has outgrown not only the primordial religious myth of otherworldly salvation but also any possible interpretation of the myth. Modern society thus not only is secular and nonmythological but it is spiritually unidimensional: it sees life and reality as all on one level — the finite. The appeals of Tillich and others of his generation to the "depths of life" invoked by the "meaning" of the old myths are expressions of beliefs and sensibilities we no longer share. Our generation is not post-Protestant or even post-Christian; essentially it is not religious in the sense of belief or dependence on "the other world." It is the traditional religious dimension that has atrophied, not just an aspect of it that has fallen out of favor. If the word "god" keeps cropping up in our conversation, it is only because we are aware that, in Nietzsche's phrase, our culture has "murdered Him." This does not mean, however, that modern man is not, in Tillich's phrase, "incurably religious." Modern man is religious, for such religiosity is a characteristic of the evolutionary being we call man, but modern religion is horizontal, not vertical; it is concerned with values and meanings within mankind and within the finite world. Modern man has rejected any interest in or dependence upon the mythological "otherworld."

In such a situation then, only the most radical attempts to redefine and reestablish the sense of the sacred have any chance of success. We should, therefore, support the tentative experiments of the radical theologians, since the repetition of the answers of the past does not fit the new questions raised by our present situation. To speak to men who believe in no world but this in terms of "the otherworld" is to be worse than irrelevant; it is to be incomprehensible.

Since the new radicals are useful gadflies for the church, it is unfortunate that most church leaders from parish pastors to denominational executives have simply rejected and ridiculed the critiques of Hamilton and Altizer. Although dozens of books have been written by and about the new radicals, and apparently are enjoying a wide circulation among the clergy, we must observe that the general response of ministers has been one of rejection, if not outright reaction in the sense that such churchmen simply renew their claims to possess the full gospel as opposed to the demands of the radicals for reform. A whole series of volumes could be prepared out of the thousands of angry sermons preached against Altizer and Hamilton, even though the majority of these sermons were based on no better evidence than reports in the newspapers or on the basis of telecasts of interviews with the young radicals. It would seem that few clergymen are able or willing to recognize that within much of the sheer publicity-seeking of some of the radicals' statements there is an inner core of valid criticism of the theology and practices of the American Church. There are exceptions to this observation, of course. Here and there, ministers and active laymen and even executives of some church agencies have cut through the verbiage to the core of radical criticism. There are some indications that all the leaders of the church are not blind to the fact that many church members and ministers are included in that vague generality known as modern man who, we are told, has lost his sense of self-transcendence.

What is included in the message of the new radicals that is a continuation of the church's own best tradition of self-criticism? In order to answer this question we need only recall the cathartic function of the heretics and reformers of ancient and medieval times, and especially the tremendous contributions of those radically critical scholars who sought to reinterpret and undergird Protestant piety in the nineteenth and twentieth centuries.[12] In my earlier book I identified some of the most outstanding of these as Ritschl, Wilhelm Herrmann, Schweitzer, Bultmann, and Tillich. These men I called "evangelical liberals" and "great synthesizers," for they attempted to restate the faith in terms that took account of both the original content of the Christian message and the place of man in his intellectual development in modern times. Together with many other concerned thinkers, including those American theologians who began the Social Gospel movement, these scholars formed what I call the " synthetic camp " of religious thinkers. It is beyond question that these thinkers did change the image of the church's picture of itself and did affect the preaching of generations of clergymen. However, the most fruitful and radical elements of their thought were never accepted as part of the theology of the church. To this observation there are also exceptions, of which the most prominent example is the new confession of The United Presbyterian Church in the U.S.A., adopted in 1967. This denomination has attempted to update its confessions in the light of modern knowledge of the Christian tradition and in response to modern man's greatly increased sense of social responsibility. But the insight of Bultmann into the nature of the New Testament, the opinions of Schweitzer concerning our historical knowledge of Jesus, and the visions of Herrmann concerning Christian piety were, for the most part, never allowed to affect the way in which the church went about its mission or formulated its theology. The one outstanding systematic exposition of all these attempts to make Christianity relevant to the modern world was the theology of Paul Tillich. Many commentators have noted that Tillich has influenced everyone in theology to a degree but has left few, if any, disciples and has affected the creedal formulation of no church (the United Presbyterian Confession of 1967 possibly being an exception). It is amazing that men who studied under Tillich or who studied his works now occupy some of the most prominent chairs of theology and religion, pulpits and church offices and yet, for the most part, these men have become spokesmen for theological views that bear no stamp of the creative genius of Tillich and his fellow synthesizers. Bishop Pike and a small group of radicals within the church, affected more by Bishop John A. T. Robinson [13] and Joseph Fletcher [14] than Tillich, are individual exceptions to this observation. Pike is an arresting illustration of this phenomenon of resistance to the efforts of the synthesizers to "update" the church. It is symptomatic of the institutional church's resistance to change to note that Pike found himself in difficulty with his fellow bishops, who had almost certainly read most of the same books that he had. What made the difference? An obvious, although partial, answer seems to be that Bishop Pike (and those like him) listened more attentively to the secular voices that spoke of the world situation around them than did his more orthodox fellows.

In my opinion,[15] the hinge of disagreement between the acceptance of at least a portion of the new radicals' criticism of the church by some advanced liberals in the church (like Pike) and the rejection of the proclamation of the Divine Death by the majority of the clergy and church leadership lies precisely at the point of an acceptance or rejection of Tillich's doctrine of the church. Briefly stated (for I will develop this point in detail in later chapters), Tillich's concept of the church is cast into the dialectic of paradox that owes so much to Kierkegaard.

The paradox of the churches is the fact that they participate, on the one hand, in the ambiguities of life in general and of the religious life in particular and, on the other hand, in the unambiguous life of the Spiritual Community.[16]

Tillich goes on to identify these paradoxical aspects as "the sociological and theological aspects of the church." [17] The new radicals (Altizer, Hamilton, Pike, etc.) are vehement in their denunciation of the "demonic" aspect of the sociological impact of the Protestant churches on American culture. It is the refusal of so much of the church's membership to live in the visible, sociologically conditioned church in a Jesus-like ("man for others," helping) way that has led the new radicals to proclaim the death of the divinity whose worship apparently makes no difference in the worshiper's life.

As Altizer asks:

Must the contemporary Christian refuse the dark chaos of
our time? . . . Already a Kierkegaard and a Dostoevsky knew
that no suffering can be foreign to the Christian, not even the
anguish that comes with the loss of God, for the way of the
Christian is to bear with Jesus all the pain of the flesh.[18]

Of course, such views are not unique. The movement toward
man in his suffering is as old as religion, as Christian as Jesus'
healing of the sick, as universal as the work of Buddha, Francis
of Assisi, and Albert Schweitzer. Such a view of the real nature
of the church's mission owes as much to Francis of Assisi
and Albert Camus as it does to Tillich or the other synthesizers;
perhaps more to Camus, to be perfectly frank. But this vision
of the Jesus-like thing to do is a natural part of the Tillichian
vision of the meaning of the Christ-event and the church's
paradoxical nature. Only Tillich — and perhaps Bonhoeffer —
was so aware of the sociological entity that is Christendom
which almost (if not entirely) obscures the dynamics of the
Spiritual Presence that alone makes the church " Holy." [19]

Tillich's contention that the church, too, needs to accept justification by grace through faith, because of its ambiguities, is
instructive for the church today.[20] The church remains the
church only as it continually holds itself in creative tension
under the negative and positive judgments of the cross. Bishop
Pike, although not usually a Tillichian, exemplifies Tillich's attitude in his recent demand that the churches of America submit
to governmental taxation.[21] No matter what we may think of
this proposal, we cannot avoid concurring in the sociological
analysis Pike makes of many Protestant churches. In his radicality, Pike — and with him Altizer and others — is waging that
fight against ambiguity in the church which is the mark of the
power of the spiritual community, to which alone, Tillich declares, " unambiguous unity belongs." [22]

Tillich's vision of the church sees it as the concrete, manifest
aspect of the spiritual community, the community of all those
who are " twice-born " because of their receptivity to that crea-

tive Spirit who urges men's minds to unity, cooperation, reverence, and love. This community is wider than the sphere of the church with its many individual churches, embracing a "latent" host of Spirit bearers throughout the world. While the latent church concept refers to the activities of all men everywhere who seek to fulfill their humanity under the impact of the Spiritual Presence, these latent community members are known — if at all — only through the corrective criticism they level at church and state, industry and labor, education and art. Thus, the new radicals, who feel themselves to be "outside" the church, are still related to the church through the Spirit who is in them that reveals himself in their critical concern.

The Constructive Impact of the New Radicals

The major constructive thrust of the criticism leveled at Christendom by the new radicals is its impact on the thinking of theologians, pastors, and laymen who still stand within the "orthodox tradition" of the institutional churches. The very shockingness of some of the radical statements serves to clear the theological air, reminding one and all that no doctrine is so firmly established — not even the doctrine of God — that it cannot be questioned and perhaps improved upon. In addition, then, to the creative ideas that are put forward by Altizer, Hamilton, and others, the radicals have this "overplus" value of forcing more orthodox thinkers and pastors to reform the doctrines and practices of the church.

In this relation of negation and criticism, the new radicals — perhaps against the will of some of them — remain loyal to the best traditions of Christian theology. It has not been the great yea-sayers alone, but the yea-sayers in concert with the equally great nay-sayers of history, who have built up Western Christian theology and Western culture in general. Thus it is neither perverse nor falsely charitable to conclude that those who proclaim the death of God do so out of loyalty to a living God, those who denounce the present practice and traditional morals of the church do so out of allegiance to the power of love, and those who decry the "institutionalism" of the twentieth-century church do so out of a paradoxical faith in the spiritual community that exists in the here and the now in spite of the pressures of a demonic church and a secular society against this development. In summary, I want to underscore the genuine hope and love of the radical critics who — consciously or unconsciously — react out of an outraged commitment to life and love and who have had the courage to wound the church in order to heal it.

If we look about us today for expressions of an awareness of the ambiguity in which the Christian church and the individual Christian stand, and an awareness of the sense of humble responsibility that devolves on those who confess belief in God, we find it less in the traditional conservatives and liberals than in the radicals of our day. It is among the proclaimers of the situational ethic and the announcers of the death of God that the full realization of Christian ambiguity is most clearly seen. It is for this reason that I have concluded that those who preach the death of God do so in the hope that men will turn to some new and more adequate conception of the living God who judges every culture and nation. Perhaps those who criticize the church do so — as I do — out of love for the spiritual community which is always wider than the church, but should, at least, coincide partially with the membership of the church. Thus genuine faith, hope, and love may lie today in the radical critics because they realize that the point of transcendence over culture, including the church, has been missed and all but forgotten by those who have bent their gaze to the immediate and have forgotten the eternal. And thus the bitterest portion of our paradoxical situation becomes clear, too, for if the severest critics of our spiritual life are the friends of the Spirit, then the strongest apologists for the church are actually those most unconcerned about "the deep things of the Spirit."

It remains true: "Not everyone who cries 'Lord, Lord,' will

be saved" — nor will help to save others. Not even the death of the God of traditional theism has repealed the moral force of Jer. 6:14:

> "They have healed the wound of my people lightly,
>   saying, 'Peace, peace,'
>   when there is no peace."

Insofar as Christendom is so constituted of men in leadership positions that the prophetic voice of criticism *within* the church is reviled and the critique of the latent bearers of the Spirit *without* the church is ignored, then Christendom is not even to be ambiguously identified with Christianity. And, insofar as Christendom is open enough to hear — and where necessary to heed — the strident cries of the radical voices now raised in our world, then, and only then, does the paradoxical and partial manifestation of the Spirit of Truth glimmer through the stained-glass windows of the church. The sequence of movement is still Spirit-world-church, not Spirit-church-world, just as the movement of the Spirit was recorded in The Acts before there was a church at all.

It is this double response to the radical's critique — of rejection by most and acceptance by some — on the part of men in authority in the church today that we shall investigate in the following pages.

Chapter II
The Problem of Change: Reformation or Revolution?

Man Come of Age in a Problematic Present

If there is any sign of our culture, any symbol that marks us off from other civilizations and other historical periods, it is the sign of rapid change. Ours is a Heraclitean world in which everything is moving, all things are flowing rapidly, everything is changing, both within things themselves and with respect to the relationships between men, institutions, and, above all, ideas. Social change is, of course, not novel, for the West has been undergoing social change since the breakup of the great medieval philosophical-theological-political synthesis of the charismatic popes and genius-bearing theologians. In point of historical accuracy, the breakup of the Middle Ages and the coming of the Renaissance and Reformation was perhaps a period of greater culture-wide change than the rapid modification of culture since 1900. However, the changes that have been going on and are still going on in the West today are the equivalent of the breakup of an era and the coming of a new renaissance in culture and philosophy. Along with this radical shaking of the Western foundations, there have been signs of the struggle of a new reformation straining to be born. *What is at issue is the character and, indeed, the historical possibility of this new reformation.* It is the contention of this book that the institutional churches of the West today are repeating the mistakes of the medieval Catholic Church in attempting to stifle this new reformation, but with the compounded mistake of not offering a viable counterreformation of their own.

It is true that the various churches of the West have offered reformatory programs and revised methods all through the twentieth century. The entire movement which has been known since the 1920's as the "theology of crisis" advocated by Barth, Brunner, and the Niebuhrs was, and is, an attempt at intellectual and even institutional self-reformation by leading members of the Western churches. The strivings since 1946 on the part of the new conservatives to revitalize the nineteenth-century orthodox reinterpretation of Protestant orthodoxy, best seen in the work of evangelists such as Billy Graham and the publication efforts of *Christianity Today* and various conservative religious publication houses, were, and are, a sustained effort to bring about a reformation in the Protestant churches of America that would be a return to the evangelical theology of the past century. The valiant endeavors of liberals, both within and without the Protestant, Catholic, and Jewish religious organizations to effect a more humane kind of social change through the civil rights movement, through support of the United Nations and other international agencies with respect to the worldwide problems of war, hunger, and population growth, were, and are, attempts at the interior and exterior reform of the church and synagogue along the lines of a religious humanism. None of these movements is without merit, but none has dealt adequately with the philosophical shift that has taken place in Western thought under the impress of the technological advances and the knowledge explosions that have been and are going on in the twentieth century. In short, not one of these attempts at reformation is adequate in itself to capture the mind of the churches as it is found among the millions of members still in these churches, and none of them has the power to capture the imagination and allegiance of the majority of the completely secularized citizens of the Western world. Therefore, we may say that so far none of the attempts

at the reformation of the church has been viable or has had a
chance at the simple historical success that is the ultimate criterion of the worth of any movement.

The Neo-orthodox Failure

The failure of these efforts at self-correction on the part of
churchmen is relatively easy to demonstrate. In the case of the
neo-orthodox reaction to the liberalism of the Protestant
Church in general during the years 1900–1920, symbolized by
the intellectual conflict between Adolf von Harnack and Karl
Barth, and by the struggle between the modernists and the
fundamentalists on the level of church politics and Christian
education in America, the failure of neo-orthodoxy to be truly
reformatory became clear after World War II. In short, neo-
orthodoxy, by preserving the words of the Bible and by preaching in heavily Biblical language while redefining the meaning
of many of those same Biblical words, ultimately showed itself
as either confused or actually deceptive. Apparently, neo-
orthodoxy with its philosophical presupposition that there was
a split between faith and reason (seen in Barth's rejection of
philosophy) led to a type of preaching that used the words of
faith in order to convey insights and meanings derived from
extra-Biblical sources, chiefly from the rising discipline of psychology and the political tenets of social democracy. This in
itself was not a bad thing; what was bad was the problem of
understanding. Neo-orthodox preaching lacked any conception
of hermeneutic, having no integral method of Scriptural interpretation; it had no real standard by which to interpret
either the Bible or the Western religious tradition. In many
ways neo-orthodoxy confuted itself, for it refused to be either
literalistic, as the neoconservatives tended to be, or liberal in
the full sense as were modernists such as George Burman
Foster [1] in the early part of the century and the rising group
of liberals interested in civil rights who became important in
the late 1940's. Neo-orthodoxy, having founded itself on a be-

lief in a sharp separation between the wisdom of man and the wisdom of God, had no alternative except to be unclear as to the meaning of its message and program, or to become so orthodox (that is, so reflective of the theology of Protestant scholasticism and the theology of the nineteenth-century American Church) as to become irrelevant to the modern situation. It thus became as harmless as the dove without the wisdom of the serpent. Reinhold Niebuhr put the plight of neo-orthodoxy in a clear way in his famous example of how he did his preaching. He said he took the Bible in one hand and the newspaper in the other and related the one to the other. Without a clear and reasonable system of interpretation, without a hermeneutic, such preaching can only be arbitrary or at best a matter of luck — for if one thinks that the Holy Spirit will provide the bridge between Bible and newspaper in that fashion, it is clear that one considers the Spirit to be irrational, and no religious institution with serious programs can be based on the belief in the irrationality of God in his relationship to the world.

The New Conservatives and Their Failure

Perhaps the best indication of the failure of the neoconservative effort at the reformation of the church is the recognition that the post-World War II popularity of church membership and church attendance has been broken in the 1960's. For some time now the churches have been experiencing a decline in membership which, while still small, seems to be statistically significant as an indication of future trends. Attendance at church is also down, especially among people under twenty-five years of age, but more important is the fact that most American denominations are experiencing difficulties in raising the large amounts of money their huge programs demand. This may be a very unspiritual assessment, but it is the assessment that the neoconservatives themselves make. The evangelical revivals and crusades have always stressed the number of conversions recorded, and the churches always make a great deal of their membership gains and losses; they struggle to pass large budgets and then fund them by intensive work among their congregations. In a more theological vein, the teachings of the neoconservatives reveal themselves to be absolutely irrelevant to the spiritual concern of modern man. The witticism that changes the name of *Christianity Today* to "Christianity Yesterday" is not without point. The "Pen-ultimate" column, entitled "Evangelical Springtime," of *The Christian Century* for April 26, 1967, reports an interview with Billy Graham that illustrates the lack of either insight or courage on the part of the neoconservative:

Evangelist Billy Graham was interviewed recently in San Francisco. With indomitable courage, Graham spoke out on several controversial issues:

On capital punishment: "I take no position."

On therapeutic abortion: "That's a complicated question, I'm not going to get involved."

On whether he approves of a bill to restrict the teaching of evolution in California public schools: "I'd have to see the bill."

On whether the Southern Baptist Convention should join the National Council of Churches. "I'll leave that to the Southern Baptists."

On Vietnam: "We ought to leave this to our leaders — they know the facts."

[On] the real problem in America today . . . : the nation's leaders are "not meeting [youth's] moral needs." [2]

Unfortunately, the neoconservative movement has identified itself all too often with social and political convictions that are, at the least, right of center. I say "unfortunately" because not all the neoconservatives could be or should be considered reactionary in their social and political views. However, the bulk of the supporters of this self-styled revival of the old-time religion are Southerners, Midwesterners and Southern Californians who hold views that disagree sharply with most of the progressive and humanitarian movements of our time. The neoconservatives are noticeable by their absence from involvement in the civil rights movement, their criticisms of the war policies of the United States Government in the 1960's, and of the attempts to involve the disenfranchised, the poor and the Negro in the labor movement and in the political processes of America.

Those churchmen and theologians who consider themselves orthodox often accuse the liberal of not having a point of transcendence in his theology, questioning whether those who place such a great stress on social and political activity in this world really believe in the existence of some higher order of reality such as the Divine (and, of course, some liberals still do so believe). Some of these criticisms of the liberal efforts at reformation have indeed been valid, but the decisive point is that the neoconservative revival (and especially the fundamentalist of the sect-type group and the rigorously "orthodox" Lutheran and Presbyterian who are often associated with the neoconservative) is actually a movement that without parallel lacks any sense of or point of transcendence above the present American cultural situation and the nation as it exists in our time. Of course, the neoconservative and others like him do not worship all the elements in our culture, nor do such thinkers worship the nation as it is; rather, they are selective and elevate those reactionary and traditional elements in our culture and nation which fit comfortably into their world view and treat these as their ultimate concern. In a real way neoconservatism, like the fundamentalism that is so similar to it (although it seeks to define itself over against fundamentalism), is an idolatry of those middle-class and essentially nineteenth-century elements within American culture which are no longer viable or helpful in our time.

Elsewhere [3] I have advanced the opinion that ours is an era in which the sense of self-transcendence is disturbingly missing from the experience of most men. Ours is a radically immanentist age, an age that finds its ultimate concerns in the here and now, in the problems of our culture and our world, and finds its hope in the youthful spirit of courage, brotherhood, and social sensitivity. Ours is an age in which a general sophistication — due to the spread of education and the effects of the mass communication media — has demythologized all myths: social, economic, political, literary, and religious. Ours is an age that is concerned with the immanent because the process of the deliteralization of man's myths has been the expression of the meaning of those myths in psychological and sociological terms. Even when men of our time remythologize, as is the case in the advent of a new and optimistic religious sensibility such as is seen in the " death of God" movement, or in the new symbols of the political movement called the new left, or the symbols of the so-called " Great Society," this remythologization is done with tongue in cheek. The reason why the younger group of radicals (who are everywhere: in the church, in labor movements, in politics, in the civil rights and peace movements) look upon the older generation with amusement is that the young understand the ironic, tongue-in-cheek quality of the new symbols and the old do not. As Bob Dylan has it in *Highway 61 Revisited,* " Something is happening and you don't know what it is, do you, Mr. Jones? " [4] What is happening is the great conspiracy of the sensitive who create symbols and do not take them literally while the insensitive react in horror at those symbols such as " the death of God " and " turning on, tuning in, and dropping out," which are broken symbols understood in a radically naturalistic way by those who use them. The failure of the neoconservative to speak to the sophisticated culture of our day is proven prima facie, for the conservative continues to use his words and symbols in a more or less literal way and accepts the words and symbols of others in the same unsophisticated sense, and so totally fails to communicate with anyone who possesses imagination.

The " age of man come of age " is the age of Freud and Tillich in a thoroughgoing way. Ours is an age of empirical sensitivities, of naturalistic and socialistic loyalties, and of a refreshingly tongue-in-cheek remythologization of various social elements of the recent past, such as pop art, op art, the stories of J. D. Salinger, the James Bond books and movies and their copies, plus the consummate corniness of Batman television shows, and movies such as *The Tenth Victim, Blow-Up,* and *Georgy Girl.*

The fact is that young people today are more politically conscious, and in general more culture conscious and thus more sophisticated, than we people over thirty — unless such sophistication has been won by us at the expense of a higher education at a large university. Young people today tend to see the self-seeking and the class bias in every political program and in every movement of the middle-class church toward the world of the university and the slum. Quite simply, our young people are more liberal than we are, and many are frankly radical in their assessment of the world.

There is, therefore, a gap between the younger and the older, a gap that becomes apparent in the middle thirties in most people — a gap of knowledge as well as a gap of sensibility. The older analysis of class consciousness simply has to be revised. Today there are only two classes, looked at from the point of view of revolutionary class consciousness: the younger and the older.

Dietrich Bonhoeffer's "mankind come of age," for the most part, embraces men and women who are barely at the legal age for voting. All of us now alive do not live in the same historical era. As Altizer says, "those who share our destiny" have a radical vision — that is, live in 1968 — and those who do not share this radical vision do not live in our destiny. Briefly put, they live in an "older era," either in the Eisenhower years, or in the Wilson years, or in the Jefferson Davis years, but they do not live in the eternal now that has dawned with the rising to consciousness of man's sense of historicity

(Heidegger, Jaspers, Bultmann, Tillich, and Dilthey) and that culminates in man's vision of the world as a piece of "equipment" (Heidegger) to be manipulated for man's cultural elevation. Other eras acclaimed the heroes who conquered the polar regions by their suffering. Our era has already conquered the poles and will soon conquer space itself through technology and superior equipment. No one can write the philosophy of our time if he ignores Cape Kennedy.

That is why the young tend to be optimistic, while the older tend to perpetuate the Spenglerian, Barthian, neo-Kierkegaardian pessimism we call existentialism. William Hamilton has spoken of this difference of attitude in his article "The New Optimism — from Prufrock to Ringo." [5] The symbols for this difference are, on the one hand, probably any recent edition of *Playboy* magazine, *The New Republic,* or *Ramparts;* and on the other, *Christianity and Crisis, Christianity Today,* and even *The Christian Century.*

The gap of understanding between older generations that have embraced neoconservatism, or that have remained in the neo-orthodox tradition, and even many of those who quite rightly consider themselves to be liberal in their apprehensions of the social and political realities of our time, is nowhere more clear than in the disaffection of the older people of America (beginning even in the '30s) from those avenues of thought which most excite the young. The very terms "LSD," "new left," or "death of God" are almost surely to be greeted negatively by those who consider themselves adult. And beyond this there is the sharp disagreement of the average middle-class churchgoer with the clergy who feel that the church should take part in the struggle for human rights and peace. Many of these churchgoers simply fail to see the inner necessity of the church's involvement in social and political issues, which is as much the fault of the clergy who should have educated them as it is the fault of the selfish mentality produced by the capitalistic spirit of America. This widespread disaffection, which is readily seen in the efforts to curb the activities of the National Council of Churches by conservative church-men, is the ultimate indicator of the failure of both neo-orthodox and neoconservative preaching to make the Christian faith relevant to the problems of human sinfulness and suffer-ing in our day.[6]

Earlier we identified the basis of neoconservatism as an idolatry. We have called it the elevation of certain elements in our culture and nation to the status of ultimate concerns. In a much stronger way the arch-reactionary elements that make up the fringe of neoconservatism do constitute a kind of right-wing church that would effect the reformation of the Christian church by absorbing all other theological positions and insti-tutions into itself, forming a kind of universal sect that would raise fundamentalism to the status of a universal theology and make America the archetype of the right-wing Kingdom of God on earth.

The Origins of Right-Wing Ideology

Prof. Edward Carnell, a very sound and intelligent repre-sentative of the neoconservatism discussed above, defined the mainstream of American Protestant fundamentalism in the fol-lowing words:

Fundamentalism is an extreme right element in Protestant Orthodoxy. Orthodoxy is that branch of Christendom which limits the basis of its authority to the Bible. Fundamentalism draws its distinctiveness from its attempt to maintain status by negation. . . . But in due time fundamentalism made one cap-ital mistake. This is why it converted from a religious move-ment — to a religious mentality. . . . It failed to develop an affirmative world view.[7]

Charles Harvey Arnold, head librarian of the University of Chicago Divinity School, has identified this type of theology as a "fundamentalism of the Word." Based on a belief in the in-errancy of the Bible and culminating in the life of believers in a Biblical "behaviorism," it expresses itself in such titles as "brother" and a stress upon a conversion experience, and makes much of the separation between the saved person and the world.[8]

In my opinion this extremely conservative theological world view is actually a carry-over of the evangelical conservatism that characterized most Protestant denominations in the late nineteenth century. Seen in this light, fundamentalism does indeed preach the "old-time religion," but it is not the old-time religion of the primitive Christian church as most fundamentalists would like to maintain.

The theological standards that mark off fundamentalism from the more progressive theology of the major Protestant bodies in America include the famous five fundamentals, proclaimed by Lyman and Milton Stewart in 1909: (1) the inerrancy of Scripture; (2) the deity of Christ; (3) Christ's virgin birth (understood literally and physically); (4) the substitutionary theory of the atonement (often called "the Blood Atonement"); and (5) the physical and literal resurrection of Christ.

We are not concerned to deprecate the religious beliefs of those conservative Christians who hold to the above-named doctrines, insofar as their conservatism is simply religious and not a cloak to cover extreme right-wing political and social views. The controversy undertaken here is with those individuals who are right wing in *all* aspects of their thinking and who use appeals to religiously conservative views to attempt to block the growth of liberal political democracy and more just social institutions because of their commitment to segregation, anti-Semitism, and other nonreligious doctrines. We are concerned here to analyze the fact brought out by Professor Carnell that so much of the effect of fundamentalism has been the development of a distinct type of negative and aggressive conservative mentality. I would like to characterize it as a form of peculiarly American religiosity.

American Culture Religion: The American Shinto

The kind of American religiosity that I see underlying the convictions of the "church on the right wing" has been described by many religious thinkers, but it is particularly clearly characterized by Gabriel Vahanian in his 1961 work, *The Death of God*. Vahanian (and of course other sociologists of religion) identified the piety of the so-called religious revival of the 1950's as "religiosity in general," which is characterized by two distinct emphases. They are: the practice of speaking of God anthropomorphically and sentimentally, and the fact that this religious language expresses an understanding of the self and its relationship to other selves, the world, and God, which is immature and selfish.[9]

The church on the right wing is not the church of those who are sincerely trying to hold to a nondemythologized Christianity, but is, in my view, the institutionalized embodiment of the inherent religiosity of a portion of the American people. Right-wing theological views reflect the self-image and self-interests of the segment of the American people that refers to itself as "Anglo-Saxon," or, in the terms familiar in the civil rights struggle, as "White, Anglo-Saxon Protestants," or "WASPs." As such, the theology of the right wing is the depository of all the values that the American people have held dear in the decades preceding the emergence of the United States into world history and into the international complications of the modern world (roughly after 1917). Therefore the right-wing church "baptizes" the ideals and self-identification of the white, northern-European-descended Protestant minority of the American people, identifying racial segregation, "states' rights" and "rugged individualism" as Christian principles. The church on the right wing thus identifies itself as a cultural religion, as the religiosity of a part of our national population rather than as a true representative of the Christian faith.

The hard core of right-wing doctrine becomes glaringly evident in such publications as *Christian Economics,* which identifies the *laissez-faire* economic principles of the nineteenth century as an expression of the Christian kerygma. This "newspaper" apparently views the United States Federal Government as the incarnation of the whore of Babylon pictured in Revelation, for it eulogizes the absence of governmental regulation as the Christians' ideal and denounces the increasing federal presence in the regulation of intranational affairs as the work of Satan — and identifies the outmoded nineteenth-century economic order with the basis of Christian faith so that it produces the fanaticism of the Southern (and Midwestern) right-winger, who is a states' righter (or isolationist) in his political views.

The ideology of the church of the right wing is a matrix of theological, sociological, economic, and political forces and tendencies that are compactly joined together by their common negativity in regard to America's participation in the world of the second half of the twentieth century, and in their common nostalgia for "the lost Eden" of a simpler day in theology, politics, and economics.

This common denominator of negativism (a reactionary outlook) concerning the modern world and a nostalgia for a "simpler day" is evident in the publications and public pronouncements of the chief figurehead of the church on the right, Carl McIntire.[10]

Carl McIntire has had a long history as a right-wing "religious" leader, emerging on the theological scene in the 1930's during the split between the "liberals" and "conservatives" of the Presbyterian Church. He has spent over thirty-five years spreading disruption and dissent among Presbyterian clergy and laymen. No problem has arisen in any Protestant body that he has not sought to exploit in his fight against "modernist" churches that belong to the National Council of Churches. In opposition to the National Council of Churches, McIntire founded the shadow organization, The American Council of

Christian Churches, and in opposition to the World Council of Churches he founded The International Council of Christian Churches. His perversity can be seen in his attempts to confuse the public and the press by holding conferences of his own groups in the same locations and at the same times as the original organizations. In the late 1950's and early 1960's there was a movement among Presbyterians to effect a merger between the Northern and Southern branches of that communion, a split that dates from the Civil War. McIntire entered the South armed with pamphlets and broadcasts in an effort to disrupt this reunion, and seemingly succeeded (at the time) as the motion to merge with the Northern church was defeated in the Southern presbyteries.

Nowhere is there more opposition to the National Council of Churches today than in the South. Without doubt much of this opposition stems from McIntire's efforts. Especially along the coastal plains and in the tidewater area there is a preponderant opinion (among white church people) that the National Council of Churches is "soft on Communism," if it is not actually Communist-inspired. Of course, the people who say this, whether Lutheran, Presbyterian, or what-have-you, also believe that the civil rights movement was thought up in Moscow. But the fact is that McIntire (and men like him) has fanned the flames of conservative resentment against the social change brought on by the 1954 civil rights decision of the Supreme Court (and subsequent decisions) and directed that resentment (now crystallized into hate) against the National Council of Churches.

The kind of reformation desired by right-wing Christians is fairly clear. It is the subjugation of all serious thought to an unimaginative fundamentalism and the implementation of a social counterrevolution that would bring the middle-class elements of the South and Midwest into power in America. Of course, no such reformation or revolution is possible. Despite the claims of such fundamentalists, the United States is not a

Christian country, and the majority of our citizens do not take old-fashioned religion and morality that seriously — which is a fortunate thing for the Christian church. Thus we cannot look for any assistance in the genuine reformation of the church from the right-hand wing of the theological spectrum.

The Neoliberals and the Death of the Civil Rights Movement

What of the reformatory possibilities of the neoliberals who have done such excellent work in the civil rights movement, in the forging of a viable method of fruitful interaction between churches and government and in extending the benefits of democracy to the poor among minority groups and in large cities? It is here that one would naturally look for the cutting edge of the Spirit's work in our culture. It is here that one would expect the most openness to new ways of being Christian. It is among these kinds of people that we would expect the need for reformation of the church to be most keenly felt since they obviously feel the need for a transformation of American society. We are not disappointed when we examine the words and works of the liberal clergy and laity. They do seem to feel the need for a new reformation. Many of these liberal leaders, such as the late Martin Luther King, did call for the revitalization of the church. For a decade, victory followed victory for the forces best symbolized by the attractive figure of the now martyred Christian Gandhi, King. However, the last few years (since 1965) have given indications that the neoliberal wing may not be strong enough to complete its work of changing secular society much less having the strength to take on the larger job of reforming the church of the West. It is painfully clear that despite the passage of several strong civil rights bills, and the increasing number of people who have gained the insight that the equality of the Negro is demanded by any reasonable understanding of the Christian faith, and is explicit in the American Bill of Rights, the civil rights move-

ment in the South is dead and in the northern cities has been
blunted if not shunted aside to extraneous concerns. The leadership of the civil rights movement, at least on its cutting edge,
has passed from the liberal to the radical. Stokely Carmichael
and those like him have replaced men like Martin Luther
King. This may not be a defeat for the Negro, but it is surely
an unfortunate thing for those who believe that the church and
dedicated Christians should be at work and in positions of
leadership in the struggle for equality. In a very real way, the
diminishment of the power of Martin Luther King (and others
like him) in the middle sixties is a diminishment of the influence of Christianity on this important element of twentieth-
century life. The victorious power of America's love for Martin
Luther King, seen on the occasion of his tragic death, may
mean that Christianity still has a chance to reconcile black and
white in America.

With the increasing power of the radical in civil rights activities and the continuing growth of radical thought in America, especially among the academic communities that increasingly play a larger and more important role in the formation of
opinion and the direction of public policy in America, the
"new left" becomes of more crucial interest and concern for
those who look for the reformation of the church. Despite the
irreverent tone of much "new left" thought, and the admit-
ted social destructiveness of some of it, the church dare not
allow the younger generation of radicals to develop a sense
of alienation from the Christian tradition, for many indicators
tell us that the future will be highly colored by this kind of
thought. The church, taken as a whole, has failed to meet the
demands of modern thought and modern problems, both in
Europe and in America, in the first half of the twentieth century. This failure is not mitigated in the least by the hasty
and often superficial efforts of denominational leaders to reform their churches and teachings in the past fifteen years in
the areas of attitudes toward war and civil rights. It is largely

because such a large number of Christians were hostile or indifferent to the call of moderate and traditionally liberal leaders who were struggling for the attainment of human rights that the civil rights movement has been marked by so many episodes of violence and that these liberal leaders have lost their power to influence the direction of this movement in the future. The church today dares not fail to come to the support of those who are calling for a rededication to human values and who work to realize those values in our society, as it has so often done in the past.

What Elements Make Up the Demand for the New Reformation?

We will investigate the nature of the radical movements of our day in the chapters that follow, but briefly here, we may say that change, radical change, will be the decisive experience of tomorrow and the other tomorrows that will make up the last half of our century. This change will give a spice and flavor of excitement to the existences of those of us who have the faith and courage to live in tension and doubt. It will be a time, in the words of Eric Hoffer,[11] of ordeal for those who must feel some absolute principles and unchanging structures undergirding their lives. Everything is now in question and will continue to be in question, and the church will have to learn to live with that dark and creative element of doubt which Tillich told us is included in all genuine faith. If there is to be a new reformation of the church, and there must be, if the church is to remain the spiritual community, all members of the church must be open to the problems that surround them and be receptive to a feeling of social unrest and moral discomfort that now marks the sociological radicals. Perhaps a Biblical and historical insight might tell us that such a restless discomfort was the mark of the demon, the voice of God, in Socrates, and the mark of the Spirit's presence in the Hebrew prophets, and in the Galilean who declared that he had come to cast fire on the earth and was frustrated until the fires of renewal were kindled in the land.

To refuse the call for reformation in the church, then, is to refuse the movement of the immanent Spirit who is the worldly presence of the silent and transcendent God.

Chapter III
The Point of Institutional Concern

W E OBSERVED EARLIER that Protestant Christianity in America has an unconscious, nonreflective but nevertheless real self-image of itself as the conscience of the state. This self-image of its moral-guardianship role is not related to the state conceived of in theoretical, that is, philosophical, theological, and legal terms, but in terms of a moral guardianship over all the citizens of the state. The Protestant Church recognizes, of course, on the popular as well as the theological level, that the state, like Jesus' conception of the church, is a mixed net of good and bad fish; a field full of both wheat and tares. This is to say only that churchmen recognize that ours is a fully secular and pluralistic society, made up not only of the heralded Protestant, Catholic, and Jewish communities [1] and their various shades of hangers-on, but also of atheists, agnostics (of several types), Marxists, Maoists, Black Nationalists, naturalists, materialists, *et al.*, most of whom have no wish to be protected or instructed by self-appointed ecclesiastical moral guardians. The ecology of society in the United States is secular, and the prying, upsetting working of the Protestant social conscience only serves to disturb the delicate balance that obtains among the various organisms that live in it. Any major statement on social or moral problems by a churchman is sure to earn a quick reaction from the secular areas. The end result of such social pronouncements by individual churchmen or by church groups is very often a stimulus to a counterreaction and results in as much harm as good for the overall social order.

The Relationship of Protestant Religion in America to American Culture

America — the "America" of the great middle class of the United States of America — has had a kind of "love affair" with the Christian religion (the Protestant variety) for some eighty years. As in most love affairs, both parties have influenced each other and from time to time have become indistinguishable from each other. Again, as in most affairs, both parties have passed through periods of mutual repulsion — the other side of their strong attraction. Like the mystery of holiness itself, the church has both fascinated and repelled American society — in some cases (as in the prohibition experiment) at the same time. Symbols of this attraction and repulsion are, on the one hand, the Supreme Court decisions concerning religious exercises in public schools,[2] and, on the other, the addition of the words "under God" to the pledge of allegiance. The pendulum swings back and forth — only loosely contained within the basic charter of the land that declares that Congress shall make no law concerning the establishment of religion.

The mutual attraction of America and Protestant Christianity is quite understandable. Both systems of thought and life are admirable expressions of the human spirit that strongly support many of the best impulses and desires of the human race. But the attraction of Protestantism in America for the American social order goes deeper than this mutual admiration, for even a slight acquaintance with American history reveals the fact that Protestantism and the American social and political order are interrelated. In brief, the love affair is one between cousins.

It is this kinship of the Protestant Churches of America with the American social and political order which has contributed to the institutionalization within the churches of so many of the human aspirations and national characteristics of the American people. The modern Babylonian captivity of the church, at least of its American Protestant branch, has come about, therefore, not by forceful subjugation but by a process of inter-related developments. The church in America emerged into modern times at the end of the nineteenth century (the period of its first great growth in the United States) as the spokesman of — and indeed the bulwark of — middle-class morality and white social power in the Eastern, Southern, and Midwestern regions of the United States.

The above observations are not difficult to substantiate. Many scholars have written of the close association of the Protestant Church and the developing institutions of the United States. Perhaps the best brief treatment of this phenomena is *The Puritan Heritage: America's Roots in the Bible,* by Joseph Gaer and Ben Siegel. In this important work Gaer and Siegel discuss the cultural impact of Biblical concepts — mediated through the early Anglo-Saxon settlers known as Pilgrims and Puritans — upon the government, law, education, medicine, and literature of the United States.[3] The authors maintain that the heavily Biblical ideals of the Puritans, though greatly modified today, are still the most influential fundamental concepts that undergird the ideas, practices, and goals that are usually considered characteristically American. They insist that ignorance of the Biblical heritage mediated through the Puritans to all later generations of Americans is also ignorance of what it means to be an American.[4]

While the great experiments of the Puritanical Calvinists to found a theocracy in New England began to wither away by the end of the seventeenth century, their desire to found the laws of the newly developing American communities on the ethics of the Old and New Testaments has never been fully lost. The restriction of the franchise to church members in good standing (which was practiced in Massachusetts) has long since been abandoned, and the right to vote extended to the Negro and even to women; but the blue laws designed to preserve the sanctity of the Sabbath are still with us in hundreds of communities all over the United States. The Puritan emphasis on morality is still very much with us, although it sits quite uncomfortably on the shoulders of modern secular man.

Many theologians and sociologists have recently written about the Protestant work ethic that is such a large factor in the American character. This is an undoubted inheritance from the Puritans and from the other Protestant sects that established themselves so fully in America.[5] The scholar Max Weber has established the connection of the Protestant work ethic, which stressed the holiness of work and the obligation of every individual to work and to contribute to the community, in his study *The Protestant Ethic and the Spirit of Capitalism.*[6]

The Counterinfluence of American Society on the Protestant Church

Edward A. Feaver, writing in *Skandalon 2*, the quarterly organ of the Student Interracial Ministry, says: " The churches symbolize the system, forgetting that Christ symbolized opposition to the system. I do not see, at this point, how this can be changed without working outside the churches, forcing them to see their captivity." [7] This is a startlingly clear and genuinely real insight. The churches are in a kind of captivity, and only a new reformation will break their chains.

The almost complete assimilation of the mentality of the Protestant communicant to a kind of " American Shinto " in which the values of the community have very largely displaced any peculiarly Christian values is vividly demonstrated in Victor Obenhaus' *The Church and Faith in Mid-America.*[8] In this fascinating study of the religion of a typical Midwestern county, Obenhaus explores the supposed differences between Catholic and Protestant Christians and between Protestants of different denominations. While Obenhaus certainly does not claim that his study of one county gives any reliable information about the religious situation throughout the United States, he cites several scholars whose studies tend to show that his findings in mid-America are also generally true of the rest of the nation. My own experiences and observations also tend to support the view that Obenhaus' findings are as pertinent to urban and Southern communities as they are to small towns in the Midwest.

The Sectarian Image of the Church in America

In short compass, Obenhaus sought to discover whether H. Richard Niebuhr, in his influential work *The Social Sources of Denominationalism*,[9] was correct in saying that the denominational fragmentation of the Protestant Church in America "represents the accommodation of Christianity to the caste-system of human society." In many respects Obenhaus' findings do support Niebuhr's indictment, showing that class, national background, and educational differences tend to determine one's choice of denominational affiliation. But, much more damaging than this corroboration is Obenhaus' discovery that there are few real theological and ethical differences between members of different denominations. There appears to be a kind of lowest common denominator Protestantism, and this denominator is extremely low in terms of Biblical and theological knowledge or social concern.

Here Obenhaus' findings illustrate one of the fascinatingly unique characteristics of American Protestant Christianity. Most sociological and historical studies of the structure of religious bodies make the distinction between the "church type" and the "sect type" of religious groupings. H. Richard Niebuhr discusses this differentiation, citing as evidence the writings of Max Weber and Ernst Troeltsch.[10] The "church type" of religious group is that which is a natural social group usually made up of people of the same racial and/or national

background and social type. It is akin to the kind of group we
see in the family and has similarities to the form of organization we encounter in a nation. People are born into a church-
type group, and membership in a church is obligatory upon
those who are born into families that are part of a church. A
person has to declare himself out of a church, for he is automatically in if his parents belonged. The "sect type" group
emphasizes an opposite tendency in religion. The sect emphasizes the separateness of the members of the religious group
from the members of society at large. There are demands that
must be met before an individual can join a sect, for he is out
until he meets the requirements and elects to be included in
the sect. Usually some type of religious experience is required
of those who would become members of a sectarian-based religious organization. The theology and the work of the church
and the sect are considerably different also. In the church the
universal aspects of the gospel, the call of Christ to all men,
is stressed. In the sect, to the contrary, the heavy demands laid
on one by belief in Christ are underscored. A strongly individualistic and strictly ethical code is mandatory for the sect's
members.[11]

The Amalgamation of Sect-Type Ideology
and Church-Type Pretensions

One of the most unusual features of American Protestant life
is the confluence of many of the aspects of the church type and
the sect type together in the typical American Protestant congregation. This confluence has been due quite as much to the
political, economic, and social situations in America as to the
genius of the American Protestant Church itself. In America it
became impossible for the pure church type of religious organization to flourish because there was no national church
that provided the necessary finances from the common treas-
ury of the people. Thus American Protestantism, after the time
of the New England experiments in theocracy and after the

disestablishment of the Anglican Church in Virginia, South Carolina, and other Southern colonies, had to turn to the solicitation of private, voluntary financial support from those who wished to become members of a given congregation. A person was not automatically a member of a church because he lived in a given community but because he freely chose to join a congregation, support it with his money, and rear his children in its faith. Here the sect type of basis for the formation of a congregation became a vital and necessary factor in the development of even extremely church-type religious groups such as the Anglicans and Lutherans. Therefore, the prevailing type of religious institution in America among Protestants has come to be a congregation in which elements of both the church-type and the sect-type associations are intermingled.

Of course, the congregations of those communions which have become known as denominations reflect more of the philosophy of the church-type group than that of the sect, despite the essentially voluntary character of the congregation. In point of historical fact, it has been in America that we have found the greatest flowering of the sectarian tendency in Christianity. In the developing United States, indeed beginning long before the conception of the United States, various sect groups founded themselves on the basis of whatever classes of people were the disinherited of the time.[12] For instance, the founding of the Baptist churches in Rhode Island came about because of the exclusion of those who held Anabaptistic views in opposition to the theology of the Puritan majorty in Massachusetts. Again and again in American history every act of intolerance, and indeed every act of omission of emphasis on one of the doctrines of the church, has ushered in a new sect group. It was in the new nation with its urge to experiment with democracy that the individualistic bias that is at the root of sectarianism had its greatest expression. However, as each new sect established itself, became able to sup-

port work outside its own congregation, and secured the services of a minister better educated than the laity, the sect
group slowly matured and translated itself into a church-type
denomination. In very simplified terms we may say that the
resultant Protestant congregations in America came to have
similarities to all other Protestant congregations that far out-
weighed any superficial differences of terminology or liturgy
imposed on such congregations by the history of the theological interest that brought them into being. More and more the
Protestant congregation in America has come to exemplify
what David W. Barry calls "the fellowship of class." [13] The
Protestant congregation thus retains a basic sectarian cast that
is strangely similar to the caste emphasis of Hinduism despite
its attempts to be a church that embraces all sorts and conditions of men. On the whole the Protestant congregation is not
oriented toward the community it serves, but is group oriented
toward a portion of the community in which it exists. As Barry
says, "The membership is a selective voluntary membership,
and association by choice." [14]

On the basis of these insights it becomes possible to understand why Richard Niebuhr could say that the most segregated
institution in America was the Protestant Church at eleven
o'clock on Sunday morning. It also becomes possible to understand why it is these present-day important groups of people,
the intellectuals by virtue of their potential for leadership and
the lower classes by virtue of their numbers and simply because of their humanity, who have been most estranged by the
church in America. All too frequently the churches have been
interested only in that class of people among whom it has
found the greatest response and for whom it has become the
institutional spokesman, the middle class. These insights also
help us to understand the findings of Obenhaus in his study
of the Midwestern congregations. He discovered that there
was a greater similarity between congregations that drew their
members from the same class rather than for any other reason.

He also discovered that "even among church constituents of superior ability there is not any great degree of interest in, or understanding of, the church's concern for the critical issues in society." [15]

The above quotation underscores the significant gap in awareness of the social implications of Christian belief between denominational leaders (at least some denominational leaders) and theologians backed up by a small core of actively committed social-minded Christians, on the one hand, and the bulk of the Protestant community on the other. In relation to any and all social issues there is bound to be a cleavage within each communion or denomination, a cleavage that will appear somewhere along the fuzzy dividing line between the self-image of the church as the church (at least potentially inclusive of everyone in the world) and that of the sect-type group as a voluntary association of like-minded and similar people who meet high standards for individual acceptance into the sect. This cleavage may not be located in precisely the same place, nor include the same group of individuals in every case. Indeed the line of distinction between a church-type apprehension and a sect-type apprehension of what Christianity means varies from social issue to social issue. It is a cleavage that runs squarely through every denomination in America (including the Roman Catholic) and in many instances runs directly through a local congregation. It is not unknown that this cleavage, which psychologically may be called the open-minded versus the narrow-minded approach to problems, runs directly through an individual's own personality. It is not hard to document this. All Christians will react in a fairly predictable way to some severely immoral social problem, such as the bombing of a church or the use of other means of violence by any group of people in connection with sociological conflict. A distinction, however, begins to appear when public policy is debated about the solution to the underlying sociological reasons that are the causes of such violence. As an ob-

vious example we may note that there are still many Protestants who defend segregation while decrying violence. Again,
there are many Protestants who know and assert that legal
segregation is wrong but who defend implicitly, and sometimes explicitly, *de facto* segregation. The cleavage between
the open and the narrow interpretation of what Christianity
means runs through each one of us who makes up American
Protestantism.

The point of this chapter has been made by the above observation. The point of transcendence, the ultimate concern that
should be the basis of Christianity and that should certainly
include the brotherhood of all men under one divine Father,
all too often becomes transformed into an ideology that limits
the universalism of Christian faith to the point of institutional
concern, which is the class that supports the particular denomination or congregation.

This theological sleight of hand which brings the transcendence of traditional faith down to the level of the economic
and social interests of those who build the congregation is a
well-practiced art in America. Although the symbols and confessions of Protestant Christianity continue to uphold the
church as the conscience of the state, potentially embracing all
its people, the actual translations of these confessions into in-
carnate life reveal that any true point of transcendence is missing. The life of Protestant Christianity in America, both of its
right and left wings, as well as its great middle range of theology, actually conceives its transcendence as fully within the
present social order. And while denominational executives
with their recent embrace of ecumenical theology show a far
greater sense of the all-embracing nature of Christian faith and
consequently exhibit more social sensitivity in regard to the
crass human problems such as those of racial strife and the
suffering of civilians in war, they all too often are limited in
their grasp of the true range of the faith and display a narrow
nationalism (or one might say, narrow Western regionalism)

in their stance against the cold war and the war in Vietnam.

It is in reference to the international affairs of the American nation that the missing point of transcendence in American Protestantism becomes quite clear. As discussed in Chapter I, one of the major theological critiques of radical critics of the church is the failure of much of the present church leadership (and the "church" theologians who support them) to understand the ambiguous nature of the church which has both a theological and a sociological aspect. In this regard, the denunciation of the radicals who proclaim the death of the Divinity whose presence seemingly makes so little difference in the life of the worshiper is surely borne out by Obenhaus' conclusion that even intelligent Protestant church members have little interest in or understanding of that degree of awareness held by the church leadership concerning social issues. Obenhaus is charitable enough to suggest that this lack of social interest is due to the theological ignorance of the Protestant churchgoer and the apparent failure of the church as a teaching institution to demonstrate the relevance of the Bible to contemporary problems.[16]

Undoubtedly this situation contributes to the problem, but a more persuasive thesis appears to be that the moral common denominator of American Protestantism (which we have already declared to be very low) is actually the ideals and aspirations of the great American middle class rather than any realistic knowledge of or concern about uniquely Christian values. In short, no problem that is not an immediate problem to the middle class can penetrate the awareness of the average churchgoer, nor can he feel that the problems of those kinds of people who are not recognizably part of the church structure, such as Southeast Asians, urban Negroes, or intellectuals (who apparently want to bear the burdens of the world), are his problems as a Christian. Perhaps this most demonic of all impacts of the American national and social experience on the Protestant Church explains why far more ministers and laymen are genuinely disturbed by the honest efforts of some theologians to fashion a new approach to morality than they are by the experiences of near-civil war in the hearts of so many of our larger cities. The reason seems clear: the children of the middle class are its most precious asset and the kind of moral codes they will or will not follow are of necessarily great interest to middle-class churchmen, but few such churchmen live in the ghettos and slums, and the problems of the children there are remote and uninteresting until the disinherited attract everyone's attention by fire and riot. This may be the case, for apparently such measures are the most effective means of calling attention to the social cancers that have beset our nation. The image of the ostrich with his head in the sand immediately comes to mind. Here we have a clear-cut object lesson that teaches the theological truth that the church can only serve the world by being the church, that is, by judging all aspects of the state, and not by being a spokesman for a partial segment of the world.

The Conquest of Ambiguity by the Acceptance of Ambiguity

The love affair between America and the Protestant Church, it should now be clear, progressed to the point of marriage for a rather large sector of the American population. Something on the order of six out of ten of our citizens are affiliated with one of the great religious communions: Protestant, Catholic, or Jewish. The Yearbook of American Churches, 1967, reports that in 1965 there were 124,682,422 members of religious communions in the United States. This figure represents 64.3 percent of the population in 1965. Earlier, the Gallup poll of 1955 found that 96.9 percent of the American people identified themselves religiously with one of the communions. Of the 1955 number, 3.1 percent of Americans identified themselves as Jews; 22.9 percent as Catholics; and 70.8 percent as Protestants.[17] These figures are substantially supported by other polls which place the percentage of Protestants between 60 and 70

percent of our total population. The United States Census poll
taken in 1957 found that 66.2 percent of Americans identified
themselves as Protestants, 25.7 percent as Catholics, and 3.2
percent as Jews. These census figures refer only to a person's
self-identification with a religious communion. It does not
mean that this vast number of people are members of churches,
for something more than a sense of identification is required
in Protestant churches for a person to be counted as a member
in even the most church-type of American denominations. In
point of fact, a far lower percentage of American citizens are
active in their attendance of and support of religious institutions. A Gallup poll in 1954 found that 79 percent of American
adults answered in the affirmative the question as to whether
they were members of a church.[18] The *Yearbook of American
Churches,* 1967, reports that a sample poll of civilian adults
taken each year between 1960 and 1965 reveals that in 1960,
47 percent of American adults claimed to have attended church
on an average Sunday, a percentage that declined over the
next four years. In 1961, 47 percent also claimed to have attended church; 1962, 46 percent; 1963, 46 percent; 1964, 45
percent; and in 1965, 44 percent. Thus church attendance
would seem to be decreasing.[19] An earlier poll by Gallup found
that in 1955 only 42 percent of those who considered themselves to be Protestant claimed to have been in church on the
previous Sunday.[20]

These figures about church attendance are even more interesting when compared to the figures of actual church members
expressed as percentages of the total population of the United
States. In 1950, 57 percent of the population identified themselves as belonging to a religious communion; in 1955, 61 percent; in 1960, 63.6 percent; and in 1965, 64.3 percent. Thus we
see that the number of persons claiming to be church members in America actually increased in comparison to the number of people in the total population, increasing by 0.7 percent between 1960 and 1965, while the number of adults in the

population who claimed to have attended church on an average Sunday declined by 3 percent during this same period. Perhaps a good average figure to work with is this — less than one half of that 60 percent [21] of Americans who claim to be Protestant are really related to the church in some significant way. Such a conclusion makes the fact that over twice as many people will claim to be Protestant even though they are not seriously engaged in church activities even more important for our purposes. The fact seems to be that Christianity is understood by most Protestants (and definitely by at least half of them) to be equivalent to living a decent life as an American citizen. There is apparently in the minds of those who think of themselves as Protestants but who do not relate themselves significantly to the church little in the message of the church that differs from average good citizenship.

If the above conclusion has any merit, we would be justified in saying that the spirituality of most of the Protestant community is deficient. It would seem that the spiritual community that Christian tradition and theology has proclaimed as the real essence of the church is not to be found in any clear way in the present Protestant Church. The ambiguities of life to which everything human is subject would appear to have overwhelmed anything distinctive in the Protestant witness. In the metaphors of Will Herberg there apparently has evolved a kind of religiosity in America that is first of all the religiosity of what it means to be a completely Americanized American and is only secondarily concerned with whether one is a Protestant, Catholic, or Jew, or even none of these, but simply an American. No one has surveyed this phenomenon better than Herberg, who has written:

Nor, on the other hand, can there be much doubt that, by and large, the religion which actually prevails among Americans today has lost much of its authentic Christian (or Jewish) content. Even when they are thinking, feeling, or acting religiously, their thinking, feeling and acting do not bear an unequivocal relation to the faiths they profess. Americans think, feel, and act in terms quite obviously secularist at the very time that they exhibit every sign of a widespread religious revival. It is this secularism of a religious people, this religiousness in a secularist framework, that constitutes the problem posed by the contemporary religious situation in America.[22]

Herberg's assessment is apparently borne out by the findings of Obenhaus, who lays some of the blame for this situation on the religious leadership of America: "A ministry preoccupied with denominational competition or focusing on the minutiae of a limited perspective can hardly provide the long-range vision expected of the people of God. The tasks demanded of the clergyman acting as personnel manager for a local congregation may obscure the ultimate objectives of the church itself. This seems to have occurred in so large a measure that congregations simply do not expect their religious leader to provide guidance at that level." [23]

Until the Protestant churches of America fully and vocally recognize and confess (and accept) the ambiguity of their spirituality — and even the prostitution of that Spirit who is said to indwell them — no reformation is possible. If the churches refuse these insights, or refuse to act on them, then the future of the church is in doubt.

Organization-Tending

Perhaps the most definite influence of American cultural institutions upon Protestant Christianity (and hence the true relationship of culture and religion in America) is the adaptation of the national pattern of the federal union and the business corporation as the model of organization for the Protestant Church. The typical Protestant denomination is modeled roughly upon the type of political government that has developed in America and is operated from day to day in a manner that copies the operation of the federal government and the great business corporations that are such a significant part of American life. Once one has this image or model in mind, the understanding of Protestant organizational life becomes simpler. There is a national organizational headquarters with a chief executive officer. There are record-keeping and tax-gathering departments, a judiciary branch, plus welfare, educational, and supervising agencies. Added to this, the typical denomination contains a heavy weight of interest in influencing the legislative process of the secular government, alone and in concert with those larger agencies (such as the National Council of Churches) formed with the cooperation of other denominations. We note that superimposed upon these levels of interest every denomination makes efforts to establish independent educational institutions that sometimes include schools ranging from nurseries to graduate schools. This natural interest in education is also followed in the production of a large body of sectarian literature ranging from Sunday church school curricula to theological and ethical works designed for study in the graduate professional schools called seminaries.

The analogy of the federal government and the typical denomination extends even to international affairs. All but a very few religious organizations maintain a strong branch whose purpose it is to extend the size and influence of the denomination abroad through foreign or world missions. This overseas activity often involves the church bodies in legal and political disputes and agreements with the United States Government and the governments of the countries in which their mission work is undertaken. There is common knowledge that the level of acceptance and good feeling toward these missionary enterprises varies from country to country according to the prevailing feeling of the population about Americans and Westerners in general. In a nation, such as Liberia, where there is strong American influence, missionaries are held in high regard, but in countries where American influence is disliked or mistrusted (as in some of the Arab nations or in those countries which wish to remain out of the cold war), missionaries are not so readily accepted or are positively excluded. It would seem that the average Protestant denomination parallels the American governmental organization somewhat closely in function, if not in a closer way. At least many non-Americans see their activities as being more closely related than Americans would like to admit.

Within the United States itself we are presented with the spectacle of dozens of Protestant denominations (there are 222 Protestant denominations and sects in America) [24] duplicating one another's work, and even in this era of interchurch cooperation, competing with one another on a number of levels. The smallest village that could be served by one congregation is often found to support four or five congregations of different denominations, and oftentimes more than one congregation of the same denomination. Of course this wasteful duplication and quite unchurchly competition is being reduced by the increasingly strong acceptance of the ecumenical movement and a growing loyalty to what is called ecumenical theology. Nevertheless, the duplication and competition that seems inherent in the denominational system has been a major factor in the rise of Protestantism in America and is still with us despite the fact that we live in an era of good feeling between church groups. There are many relatively strong denominations that will have little or nothing to do with the efforts of ecumenical leaders to bring about increased cooperation and the possibility of union of the various church bodies. Some of these are the Southern Baptist Convention, The Lutheran Church — Missouri Synod, and indeed it appears most of the Lutheran denominations in America.[25] Recently, Dr. Robert J. Marshall, president of the Illinois Synod of the Lutheran Church in America, told the Illinois Synod meeting: "In the near future, Lutherans will grow closer together. . . . Many other Protestants will work more and more under the influence of the Consultation on Church Union. Catholics may find a place in councils of churches. Lutherans will continue to hold a distinctive place for the time being." [26]

It would appear that a statement such as that of Dr. Marshall, who is a recognized leader of the Lutheran Church in America, might indicate a reluctance on the part of the Lutherans (who are the third largest Protestant group in America) to entertain the possibility of Protestant Church unity.

The analogy of Protestant Church organization and American governmental organization becomes more realistic when we recognize that the inefficiency and the theological incompatibility of the large number of parallel denominational structures have counterparts in the great number of overlapping governmental structures in America. Recently political scientists and sociologists have grown concerned with the tragic waste of tax funds and the red tape occasioned by the competing municipal, county, state, and federal agencies in urban areas. There are an amazing number of governmental units in the United States, each distinct from one another. In fact, there are 102,392 different governmental units, which makes the Protestant fragmentation seem modest indeed. Although there are only fifty state governments, one national government, and 3,050 county governments, there are 17,215 city governments and 17,198 town governments to which must be added 50,454 school districts.[27] In a very real sense the political ideology of the American nation is responsible for the kind of emphasis on local government that is reflected in the above figures. This ideology, of the right of the average man to govern himself, runs deep in the mythology of America, although it has been perhaps as much myth as actuality in our history.[28] Although the right to local self-government is an impressive standard of belief and a valuable contribution to civilization that owes a great deal to the Anglo-Saxon people and to the American experiment, it is not necessarily the most perfect form of church government. However, the emphasis on

local government that developed in America became also the
emphasis of the emerging Protestant denominations. It is not
surprising, then, that the result of this emphasis was the large
number of sect groups that still exist.

The Church as the Conservator of Values

The incorporation of American political values in the Protestant churches is not in itself the root of the serious problems in which Christianity in America finds itself today. It was
perhaps necessary and natural that the double opportunity for
civic and religious freedom would result in a form of religion that drew from and contributed to the developing national
political consciousness. The severe problem that we have identified as organization-tending, and that we have spoken of elsewhere as an all too often reactionary attitude of churchmen
toward modern social problems, arises from the traditional
function of religion as the conservator of the values of the society in which it is set. This function is one of the great services
religion performs for man, of course. Religion becomes a great
depository for insights and sensitivities achieved by the genius
of unusual men and the struggles of the masses of men over
long periods of time. Without this conserving function there
could be no civilization, as all law codes originated and the
foundations of all educational systems grew out of the impulse
of religion to preserve and extend the insights and values of
their founders, and of the teachers and philosophers that contributed to the rise of religious and cultural ideas. To fault religion, and specifically the Protestant Church in America because
it is a great conservative institution, is to speak irrationally.
One cannot imagine the present state of human civilization
without the influence of Moses, Amos, Isaiah, Jesus, Paul, and
indeed, without Buddha, the Hindu sages, and the founders
and teachers of other now-dead and still-living religions.

Consequently, the problem of the present-day Protestant
Church does not consist in its fidelity to the conserving func-

tion of religion which was reemphasized by the Protestant founders: Martin Luther, John Calvin, John Knox, and John Wesley — to name but a few. Rather, the problem of the Protestant Church in twentieth-century America has been the uncritical impulse to conserve too many traditions and values that were of only temporary historical interest and that now either have been rendered irrelevant to man's condition or in some instances have become positively harmful to man's spiritual development. Unlike its founders, who critically judged the traditions and doctrines of the medieval church against which they were protesting, the Protestant Church of twentieth-century America has all too often affirmed and defended values that were in actuality the values of a particularly small segment of the human race over a relatively short period of time. An example may make this clearer. The various ideological viewpoints that developed in America from the time of the Revolution to the coming of that attitude of sectionalism which ended in the Civil War were often interpreted as different religious outlooks on the meaning of life.[29] It is a historical fact that hundreds of ministers and congregations of various Protestant communions defended slavery,[30] arguing from the Bible that the white race was obliged to enslave the darker races because of some terrible sin committed by Ham, the son of Noah (Gen. 9:18-29). When war approached — and indeed we might say, contributing to the coming of that war — almost all denominations split into Northern and Southern sections over the issue of slavery or the related ideological doctrine of states' rights.

In 1845 the Southern Baptist Convention was organized by delegates from the eight slaveholding states. In the same year the Methodist Episcopal Church, South, was formed because of a quarrel over a slaveholding bishop. In 1861 the Presbyterians in the secessionist states formed the Presbyterian Church in the Confederate States of America which became the Presbyterian Church in the United States, after the South was defeated. The Lutheran Church also split over the war, with the United Synod, South, being formed in the Confederacy — a division that was only healed in the creation of the United Lutheran Church in America in 1918.[31] The Methodists did not reunite until 1939, and the Presbyterians have not as yet reunited, although all Presbyterians are now taking part in the Consultation on Church Union.

In a very real way, the present-day churches that exist in the southern part of the United States, not only in those denominations which have healed the breaches of the American Civil War but also in those which remain separate,. still perpetuate some of the ideology and the social values of Southern culture in the mid-nineteenth century. Even under the unquestionable influence of the policies of the United States Government since 1954, it is apparently still possible for organizations and groups, both secular and religious, to hold meetings and make plans for the whole community while it is clear to an objective observer that only the white community is being consulted. One of the interesting features of life in the present-day Deep South is the day-to-day observation of the overlapping concentric rings of interracial and single-racial activities. It is possible to attend a movie and sit next to whites and Negroes, but it is not possible to do so in church. These observations are made out of the author's own experiences but are buttressed by the experiences of many others, that might be symbolized by the following quote from " The Death of Religion and the Rebirth of the Church," by Edward A. Feaver.

First, the churches have not participated in the secular lives of their members. They have developed an elaborate dualism between the sacred and the secular that is used as justification for this failure. This dualism is religiously defended by both black and white — especially in the South — because it protects its advocates from the unsufferable guilt that would result if the dualism ever crumbled. There is no theological justification for separating one's religious from one's social life, and preachers and their followers who cling to this separation must be corrected.

Second, the churches — white and black — perpetuate the slave system. In the name of Christianity the churches have taught people to be passive in accepting their lot (as in the case of Negroes), or to consider their social station in life as divinely ordained (as in the case of whites). Three examples will suffice to illustrate this point: (1) A white woman told me that as a Christian she could not permit integration because God had ordered some to be masters (the whites, of course) and others slaves. She went on to add that if only the Negroes were good Christians, they would not be causing all of this fuss. (2) Whites have taught blacks Christianity from a white perspective, teaching them the afterlife themes so that they would not seek the "Kingdom" here and now. Therefore several people under the direction of their brainwashed preacher refuse to participate in community activity because it is "against God's will." Everything is to be settled at the day of judgment. (3) The definition of Christian social love presented by the churches — white and black — has kept people from seeking change. Social love, as taught in the Negro churches, is supposed to equal being satisfied with one's position, seeking peace at all costs, and not being involved in the messy business of power. In the white churches, social love is defined as some sort of sentimental, romantic concern for the plight of the oppressed which usually results in charity-giving to salve the conscience of the giver. Unfortunately such charity carries with it the odious stigma of the superiority of the giver over the recipient. Such conceptions of love are actually products of a capitalist-racist system, and have little to do with Christian social love.[32]

With the rising tide of terror that has been fostered by the kind of demonization of Christianity that Feaver is attacking, a tide that is lapping higher and higher on city halls, state capitols, and even on the national capitol itself, in the late 1960's, there is no longer any time for defenses of the sincerity of churchmen who hold such views or for the prejudice of geographical schizophrenia which recognizes warped religion only in the South. What Feaver says, and what we have been saying, about Protestantism is true of every area of the United States, and there are indications that it is true of the Roman Catholic Church as well.

The Corporation as Another Image of the Protestant Church

The efficiency (if one does not mind accepting Parkinson's Law [33]) of the modern Protestant Church is amazing. The national headquaters of each denomination parallels the organization of the federal government as we remarked above, but it also parallels in spirit and in method the modern corporation. Not long ago a church agency adopted the slogan, "People Are Our Only Business," which is a kind of Freudian slip, since many such agencies approach their task in what can only be called a businesslike spirit. Of course intelligence and efficiency are needed in the church's work as well as in the business world; what we are criticizing is the professionalism and the sense of competition that is engendered by such professionalism in the church. Large church bodies are set up with budgets that are divided between various agencies and divisions not unlike the slicing up of the federal budget or that of General Motors. Once this money is appropriated, the church executives expect that a profit will be earned by its use — even if that profit is an increase in church membership or the production of better church school material rather than the accumulation of capital funds. However, churches also have divisions that do set out to accumulate funds, such as stewardship and special offerings projects or the maintenance of rather large investment portfolios. There is little doubt that the churches of America are extremely wealthy, and own and control large amounts of real estate and huge blocks of stocks and bonds.[34] Perhaps the nation is fortunate that the various churches are divided so that this huge financial holding is not in a single pair of corporate hands.

To return to the real point, however, the corporate image that the large denomination has of itself has led to several sins that are peculiar to the church. One such sin is the encouragement of time-service and the endless experimentation with and reproduction of "church programs." Again and again we are informed that a board is promoting a new program for evangelism or stewardship, only to find that it has its little day and passes on. Again we are treated to the yearly production of new educational literature — each book supposed to be more "modern" than the last. We repeat that no one denies the need for ceaseless educational activity on the part of the church. It is a part of the church's legitimate function to prepare the very best kinds of books and other teaching devices possible. What we are criticizing is the apparent endlessness of new experimental programs that may legitimately be seen as sheer busyness that results in multiplied materials which do more to confuse than to aid congregational educational efforts. If there were other kinds of criteria than sheer volume or the doing of something for the sake of doing something, this kind of situation would disappear. Unfortunately the production of masses of papers and ceaseless activity is a dominant part of the corporate image that has become one of the models of the modern church.

Donald L. Metz, author of *New Congregations: Security and Mission in Conflict,* had the image of the church as a corporation in his mind when he wrote the introduction to his important study of the sociological structure of modern Protestant Church organizations. He reinforces and underlines our thesis that the church has modeled itself on a business pattern when he writes: "If the church had been listed in the stock market over the past few decades, it would have been considered a booming enterprise. As an organization it has had an impressive growth, evident both in the enlargement of its membership and in the increasing amount of real property it controls." [35] Metz's study of six new congregations, carried out through the Survey Research Center of the University of California, used the case history method. In the course of his research, Metz points out that the congregation (and note that we are now discussing the local congregation and its similarity to a business organization), like all social bodies, must deal with problems of morale, leadership, and adaptation. The congregation has these "survival tasks" no less than the lodge, the fraternity, the department store, the governmental department, or a large corporation. In meeting these survival tasks, which for the church are the attaining of a growing membership, building a house of worship and educational facilities, and forming and raising a budget, the congregation runs into a problem peculiar to itself as a supposedly spiritually oriented body. It diverts some (if not most) of its interests and resources away from the accomplishment of its "primary goal," the creation of spiritual personalities in men.

In the case of new or mission congregations, at least, the odds are that the local church will become almost solely interested in the survival goals of building a congregation. In its necessary drive to build enthusiasm so as to erect the building and have warm bodies for leaders, teachers, and choir members, the tendency is very strong to hide or discourage any conflict between pastor and people — or between members — about the primacy of spiritual goals over the shallowness of organizational and financial considerations. The very leadership of the church, its church councilmen, elders, and/or deacons, will be selected from men who are "good businessmen" or who have or have held executive positions. Such men are certainly not to be considered unchristian, and some of them undoubtedly wish to achieve the primary or spiritual goals of the church, but all too often the emphasis is placed on those men who know how to get things done in an organizational sense rather than on those with knowledge of or loyalty to the wider meaning of the gospel. Metz's study reveals a condition that obtains in some modern mission congregations where members of the governing boards of churches completely lack any sensitivity to theological problems or issues.[36] Apart from a vague feeling that a particular congregation is and ought to be Baptist, Methodist, or Lutheran, there is little or no conception of what the symbolical positions of these communions stand for. In my experience such a lack of sensitivity is often one of the reasons for the election of church officers. At the stage where all energies are bent toward buying land and building a physical plant, many organizing groups of laymen feel that a person with a keen sense of the differences of his communion from other communions is a drawback rather than a help to the mission. This is undoubtedly because most new mission congregations are composed of a mixture of families from many different Protestant backgrounds and from many different geographical points of origin. Nothing stops the bureaucratic wheels of a church meeting or the carrying out of a program faster than a statement like, " Back in Iowa, in Christ Church, we did it this way." The end result of the efficiency of church-building lay people is all too often the creation of an organization that recognizes no other goal than the building and smooth functioning of its own organism — except in a kind of abstract way. The service of these extraorganizational goals (the spread of the gospel, support of the larger church, Christian witness in society, etc.) is often sporadic or nonexistent. Even when the more inclusive church (such as the synod, district, or presbytery) is served with financial contributions, there is often a good deal of grumbling about this " imposition " on the mission congregation, which reveals the lack of any sense that the church is greater than its local manifestation.

We may summarize by saying that the image of the church from the denomination to the congregation is all too often modeled on the governmental agency and/or the business corporation. The corporate image is frequently imposed on the quite spiritual desires of a group of local Christians for the establishment of a church by the " all-business " boards of church extension through their representatives in the field. When the purchase of property, the gathering of a required number of members, the success of a building fund drive, and the erection of a building are again and again stressed and pushed — first from the denominational agency, then from the mission pastor — there is little wonder that the outgrowth of this procedure is the mirror image of a successful business with the theology of a sect that recognizes nothing of the church beyond the limits of its parish property.

Metz's investigation in California also discovered the nature of the unhealthy state of the new congregation once it has met its survival tasks and is in its building. There is a distinct feeling of letdown, a loss of enthusiasm, and an upsurge of oftentimes petty bickering (along with the outbreak, in some instances, of real theological conflict that was suppressed earlier) in the group. The bickering and conflict often result in dissatisfaction with the minister who guided the building program, with the result that such a " church builder " more often than not moves on to a new field to remove himself from the turmoil and aid the congregation to a healthier state by the calling of a new minister. But all too many times the congregation finds no relief by this ploy, for it suddenly discovers that it has created an organizational monster that demands ever more organization-tending and more and more funds to operate. Instead of being able to shift direction away from the survival task it faced in its infancy to a more mature style of life as a cell in the body of Christ with responsibilities toward the larger church and toward society, it feels itself caught in a rigid routine of artificially maintaining its former enthusiasm so as to continue meeting its financial commitments. I have witnessed such phenomena in several states and recognize them as some of the chief hindrances to the flowering of a spiritual community. I am quite heartened by the one congregation that Metz discovered and studied which had avoided these pitfalls.[37]

In closing, it must be observed that the organization-building procedures outlined above, which result in church leadership by men of executive positions, is one of the major reasons for the continuing middle-class bias of the Protestant Church.

While there are exceptions, it must be stated that on the whole few, if any, blue-collar workers become leaders of congregations. There would be exceptions to this in the case of mission congregations begun in areas where there were few members of the denomination sponsoring the mission. For instance, in my experience in Florida, there were few Lutherans on my mission territory, and in the beginning one or two blue-collar workers were in leadership positions. However, as the membership grew, this situation changed, until the church leadership was exclusively white-collar with the top positions held by the financially most able. Apart from rural congregations which may be made up of small farmers and tradesmen, or missions among industrial communities (the famous "mill hills"), there would be few exceptions to the statement that the leadership of Protestant congregations is not only middle class but as close to the upper middle class as the structure of the community will allow. It is consequently not surprising that there is so little understanding of and concern for the poor, the Negro, or for any group that deviates from the middle-class standard, on the part of the Protestant congregation. Whatever the Protestant congregation is, it is usually not the mixed bag of " Jew and Greek, male and female, slave and free " that is revealed to us in the New Testament.

Now that we have examined the sociological state of the present-day church, and found that the spiritual impulse of Christianity often becomes blunted in the day-to-day organizational life of the congregation, it is time to ask ourselves about the more basic nature of the modern church — its theological understanding of itself. In order to gain such theological insight into what the church believes itself to be and to understand the criteria by which its most enlightened spirits judge the church, let us turn to an investigation of what some modern theologians are saying about the church and what it ought to be.

Chapter IV
A Theological Look at the Church

W<small>HEN WE LOOK</small> at the church as it exists in our cities and towns in the 1960's, we are struck by the sheer mediocrity of its intellectual, i.e., its theological, life and the busyness of its institutional life. We hear sermons extolling the place of the home and family in our national life, then we are invited to attend a multitude of meetings and events that alone (without secular "help") are enough to disorganize the most stable families. We are sermonized about the need for justice and fair play, then treated to segregated assemblies and made aware that the lay employees of the church and many of the clergy are paid below subsistence wages. Where, in all the superorganizational froth of the modern church, do we find that sense of the ambiguity of the Spirit's bearers and that allegiance to humble responsibility which is the mark of Christ's men? If we really want to find this wistful and humble attitude, we must look not to the church leadership, except in rare instances such as Bishop Pike, but — wonderful to relate — to the theologians. Those theological thinkers who are immersed in the life of the world and who, through their mastery of modern philosophical and sociological thought, attempt to speak to the world are much clearer about the nature of the church than are those who direct it on the national and local levels.

Whenever we attempt to be "theologians" and ask ourselves the question, "Where is the Spirit at work in the church?" we find the answer difficult to secure. Like Sisyphus, we seem to have taken on an unending task — if we do not succumb to discouragement first. Indeed, like Sisyphus, we may find that our craftiness in asking questions and our avarice in seeking answers have landed us in Hades! For where would you look to see the Spirit's work? Granted that you will not accept answers that have been tried and proven unhelpful, such as "in the Sacraments," or "in preaching," or "in good deeds," without further explanation. Just what is there about the church as we know it and participate in it in our time that would lead one (apart from habit and exposure to traditional words) to confess that the Divine Spirit is at work in this diverse and all too human group of organizations called "churches"?

Someone will say that this is an impertinent, if not a silly, question. Perhaps. But all too often it is just such impertinent — and silly, even childish — questions that philosophers, who want to be wise, and reformers, who want to be holy, ask, and keep on asking until they get an acceptable answer. For our part we find such evidence of the Spirit's work very unobvious, to say the least. The many commentators, conservative, liberal, and radical, who are writing books on America's present spiritual state would seem to agree.[1] Certainly the radicals have made the point that the present-day church is not the unambiguous bearer of the Spirit that it claims to be.

It is all very well to point out the weaknesses of the institutional church, for these weaknesses have been with the church from the apostolic age, but our real concern ought to be what is the criterion or basis of comparison by which we judge the church to be strong or weak? Gordon Rupp, by reference to the incident of Ananias and Sapphira in Acts 5:1-11, speaks of the dishonesty the church's members have shown to God. He goes on to compare "the feet of the young men" who carried out the bodies of these two church people who lied to God to the young radicals of today who charge the church with dishonesty.[2] Unfortunately, Rupp uses this very suggestive symbol to imply that "the young men" lack any basis on which to evaluate the church. If this were true, then we would be justified in ignoring most of what the radical theologians have said — but such is not the case. Almost all the radical critics of the church today are quite theologically adept and are influenced — to a greater or lesser degree — by the work of the twentieth-century's outstanding systematic theologian, the late Paul Tillich. Tillich most clearly was a "theologian of the Spirit" and spent much of his life's work on the analysis and description of the place of the Spirit in the church and the world. Perhaps a discussion of his description of the church and its relationship to the Spirit will help us to assess genuinely the strengths and weaknesses of the modern church.

Tillich's Concept of the Spirit or the Spiritual Presence [3]

In everyone's mind the ideas of the church and the Holy Spirit are at least closely related, if not connected. Acts 1:4-5; 2:1-21; 4:8; *et al.*, specifically equate the beginning of the church with the manifestation of the Spirit to the early disciples through an expression of power that forced them to begin preaching about Jesus in ways that attracted hundreds of men to their confession about Jesus' Christhood. From the earliest days of the church it has been assumed — and apparently rightly — that the Spirit is the true inner power and guidance of the church's life and work.

However, while the average person believes that he knows something of what a church is, not even the creeds are very clear about what the Spirit is. Numerous writers have pointed out the unclarity of the church's confession about the Spirit.[4] In the usual sense, a sense accepted by Paul Tillich and other leading theologians, the Spirit is the name men give to the presence of God in the world. The Spirit is God in the immanent dimension, as Joseph Haroutunian has said, "God with

us," [5] and as Luther has said, "God in us." [6] Unfortunately, the
traditional expression "Holy Ghost" used in English has ob-
scured even this little knowledge we have of the meaning of
Spirit, as "Ghost" has had no real meaning for English-speak-
ing men for centuries. All too often the expressions "Holy
Spirit" or "Holy Ghost" are simply repeated without understanding. To rectify this situation, Tillich made a real effort to
revitalize and renew the concept of Spirit in modern theological discussion. Tillich remarked that the word "spirit" had
been subjected to misuse over a period of many years and
consequently needed a thoroughgoing rehabilitation. [7]

In Tillich's teaching on the Spiritual Presence, spirit is used
in a twofold sense: (1) spirit (spelled with a small s) which
signifies the human spirit and which is used to name that function of life which characterizes man as man and which man
expresses in his morality, culture, and religion; and (2) Spirit
(spelled with a capital S) which signifies the Divine Spirit or,
as Tillich prefers to say, the Spiritual Presence. [8]

The important thing to remember when one is studying the
very involved thought of a writer like Tillich is that here is a
theologian who has been forced to turn into a philosopher in
order to attempt to understand how God deals with man. For
Tillich it is impossible for man to have dealings with the Spirit
of God unless man, too, is a spirit. This idea is as reasonable
as it is Scriptural, since it is very like the concept of the image
of God referred to in Genesis. In Tillich's view the term
"spirit" names a dimension of life; that is, the particularly
human realm that is seen in man through his power of self-
awareness. This power of self-criticism and self-measurement
makes it possible for man to integrate himself and become free
and creative. Through his ability to create, man has founded
culture and science and is able to transcend the conditions of
existence that bind animals to the earth. Man's spirit is not a
separate part of man distinct from his body, nor is it simply
his mind. Rather, spirit is the total man himself which we may

call the unity of man's life and the meaning of his life as he understands it. Insofar as anyone knows, spirit comes into being only in man, and for this reason Tillich speaks of man as the bearer of the spirit. Man bears the spirit in such ways as the development of his personality and uniqueness, through the ability to reason and learn, and especially through his ability to make decisions and thus show his freedom and moral responsibility.

How does the Spirit come into contact with the spirit? For Tillich as for most of the teachers of the church, there is distinction between Spirit and spirit. The Spirit is said — by Tillich on the basis of Paul — to indwell or to live in the spirit of man. This is the kind of language Paul used in Gal., ch. 2, when he referred to the Spirit of Christ which lived in him. Tillich points out, however, that the Spirit does not come into a man and merely stay there but that the Spirit puts man in motion and drives him to spiritual acts like those recorded in Acts, ch. 2, where the disciples showed courage and proclaimed Christ to the crowd.

We may well ask how the Spirit comes to man's spirit. Our answer must be that the Spirit is always present in the world and in every man, but men are not naturally aware of the fullness of the Spirit's presence. However, under the impression of preaching or of a sacrament or of an act of faith or love, men are brought to a consciousness of the presence of that Spirit who is always there but who is not revealed to them until the conditions are such that he can be recognized. This act of revelation Tillich calls ecstasy, although he does not mean that it is irrational; on the contrary, he maintains that the receiving of the Spirit heals the anxieties of man's mind and gives him a truly reasonable self.

According to Tillich's analysis, the man who has become aware of the participation of his spirit in the Divine Spirit is driven to live in a transcendent mode of life. This life in the Spirit demonstrates four aspects which should be the marks of

a member of the church if indeed the church is an agency for
bringing men to a realization of the Spirit's Presence.

The first of these aspects of spiritual life is the *increasing
awareness* of one who has the Spirit. The spiritual man becomes more and more aware of the situation in which his life
is lived, with its many problems and conflicts and ambiguities.
The spiritual man should show an increasing concern for the
gap between preaching and practice, between professions of
freedom and actual denials of civil rights, between professions
of the love of peace and actual warlike conduct. Such an
aware spiritual man will be constantly pointing to these problems, even when others are not aware that they are problems,
and he will suggest that there are possible answers to these
problems within the Christian tradition. Thus, any organization made up of such aware individuals ought to be the most
sensitive critic of its society.

A man who has been grasped by the Spirit will also show
increasing freedom. Not only will he become more and more
free from the moral law as a binder on his conduct, just as Paul
declared that the Spirit of Christ had set the Christian free
from subservience to the law, but he will also become free
from the habits and traditions and customs that bind his fellowmen in patterns of conduct that quite often bring about injustice in the name of justice and immorality in the name of
morality. It is no accident that it was Christian men and
women who first raised the issue of the evils of slavery during
the last century and of the evils of segregation in our own
times. The man who has the Spirit increases in a spiritual maturity that leads him to live by the Spirit rather than by the
letter. Such a life is one of grace rather than one of rules; it
is a religious life rather than a merely moral one. It fulfills the
law not by keeping law but by living in love.

The spiritual man also shows *increasing relatedness.* Living
in the Spirit leads a man to maturity so that he finds his own
self-identity beyond the traps of a false humility that grows

out of despair or self-hate and beyond a false pride that grows out of belief in nothing beyond himself. Because of the wholeness that the Spirit brings into our lives, there is no need to seek security by identification with ideas and groups that elevate one section of mankind over others. Having the Spirit is a proof against racial prejudice, national pride, or class consciousness. One is freed from these dead ends that lead to hostility and the very insecurity they seek falsely to overcome so that the spiritual man can creatively and openly identify himself with his own social group and with members of all other social groups in a free and open manner of friendship and respect.

Finally, the man who is indwelt by the Spirit lives a life of *increasing transcendence*. This aspect of his life is his devotional life which may indeed express itself in prayer or public worship but is hardly restricted to those specific avenues. Transcendence means spiritual freedom, an ability to get beyond oneself and one's own concerns, including the concerns of his own church, social, and national groups. In the fullest sense this is what is called by the philosophers " openness to the universe," that sense of oneness with the ground and source of everything, the Divine.

The Media of the Spirit's Presence

The question keeps arising as to just how the Spirit becomes effective and important in the life of man. One important historical answer to this question has been through the sacraments. In the systematic theology of Paul Tillich this traditional answer is retained and given added breadth and strength by a doctrine of " pan-sacramentalism," [9] by which Tillich means that throughout all history there have been historical and personal events through which the Spirit has come to be effective in human life, both in and apart from the traditional sacraments of the church. For Tillich any object in the world can become the material vehicle of the Spirit.[10] This

view must be understood not as a depreciation of the sacraments, such as Baptism and the Holy Communion, but as the
expression of a belief that is as old as Christianity that God
can work and does work when and where he wills. Examples
of events that can become sacramental might be a mother's
kiss given to a child who is hurt or afraid, a cigarette given to
an injured person as an expression of loyalty and concern, or
the inspirational qualities that may arise when a person looks
at a sunset or at the vastness of the sea. In Tillich's own life,
the sea played an important part; as a younger man he often
went to the North Sea and did his thinking while gazing out
at the water. Just because men do come to insights about themselves and God and receive courage and inspiration from such
apparently nonchurchly related events, there is a genuine
strengthening of our ability to believe in the truly sacramental
qualities of water, bread, and wine.

Tillich says that all sacramental materials, whatever they
may be, are symbolic, but that this does not mean that they
are mere signs but rather they point beyond themselves saying, in effect, that I am not just a kiss or bread or a sunset, but
I participate in the life of God. In Tillich's words these symbols participate in the genuine power of that which they symbolize. Additionally, the materials of a sacrament are usually
related in some close way with what they symbolize and express. This is clearly seen in baptism, where the material element, water, symbolizes washing and renewal.

The church or the spiritual community is bound to definite
media of the Spiritual Presence and yet these media must be
subject to the criterion of Jesus as the Christ. Nothing out. of
harmony with the revelation through Jesus can be a sacrament. Also, the sacramental act must refer to the historical or
doctrinal symbols related to the life of the Christ.

The Word of God, i.e., the Word which becomes the vehicle
of the Spiritual Presence, is not limited by Tillich to the Bible.
The Word is used by the Spirit just as sacramental media are

used. Any word can be the Word of God if it so grasps the human mind in such a way that it creates an ultimate concern for it. On the other hand, no word is the Word of God unless it is a Word of God for someone. It is important to note that no word can be the Word of God if it contradicts the faith and love which are the work of the Spirit and which is the new being manifested in the Christ.

The Man Who Experiences the Spirit's Power in His Life

In the analysis of the life of a member of the spiritual community — that is, the inner dynamic power that undergirds the church — Tillich discerns three traditional elements: faith, love, and self-transcendence. The man who has come in contact with persons and things that make him aware of the Divine Spirit in a very real and personal way will show faith. Faith is not a thing but a state — a state of being grasped by the awareness that all things came together in God. Love is not merely an action but also a state of life, a state of feeling that one has been taken into the unity of the Divine Spirit. In Tillich's usual theological language faith is the state of being possessed by an ultimate concern, a driving aim and purpose for one's life. Love, then, is the state of being filled with this passionate concern which drives one to a life of action designed to reunite all men with one another and with the Divine that underlies all of life.

Self-transcendence, or, in more ordinary language, the state of being freed from one's preoccupations and limitations so as to relate oneself openly to others and to the divine basis of life, is the aim of all religious theory and practice. In the older, pious terminology such transcendence is described as the state of salvation — or being filled with the Spirit. Anyone who lacks this transcendence lacks true religion; thus we cannot describe the church and the church members apart from the presence of such transcendence in their lives. If organizations or individuals lack this transcendence, then regardless of their opinions about themselves they are not the church or any part of it.

Tillich says this drive toward an unambiguous reunion of separated individuals with one another through participation in the transcendent unity is agape, which is the creation of the Spiritual Presence. This transcendent unity overcomes the ambiguities of life. These ambiguities are rooted in the separation and interplay of essential and existential elements in being, but in the transcendent union all separated elements are reunited; this removes the conflicts and ambiguities of the life processes so that actual being becomes the true expression of potential being — which can be fully realized only after estrangement, contest, and decision. In this reunion ambiguous life is raised above itself to a transcendence it could not achieve by its own power. This union, therefore, is the answer to the question implied in the processes of life and in the function of the spirit. In love there is an element of emotion that is the participation of the whole being in the process of reunion whether in anticipation or fulfillment. This drive for reunion belongs to the essential structure of life and is found throughout all the dimensions of life. As emotion it is experienced as blessedness in man. Without this emotional quality we would not experience agape, for agape contains the divine symbol of blessedness. Love as faith is a state of the whole person. This means that love is one under all its manifold forms and is actually the inner dynamic quality of life. However, only agape is an ecstatic manifestation of the Spirit and is possible only in unity with faith. In this respect, agape is equivalent to the new being. Agape may indeed be used to characterize the divine life itself symbolically and essentially. To speak of God as "love" is to say more about God than we might generally recognize.

The Work of the Divine Spirit in History

One of the primary features of Western religious thought and life is the belief, based on the experiences of the Hebrew people recorded in the Old Testament, that God's Spirit works in history. This is a general belief among Jews and Christians which has a good deal of acceptance in Western philosophical thought. The theology of Augustine, of Thomas Aquinas, of Luther and Calvin, of Barth and Niebuhr, as well as the philosophy of Hegel, is unthinkable without this basic belief that the Spiritual Presence has been manifested in the life of historical mankind.

However, between the more open and liberal philosophers and theologians and the more literalistic theologians, both old and new, a problem arises as to the specific place or places within history where the Spirit has made himself known. In the more orthodox, this question is answered by saying that the Spirit has manifested himself in a saving or transcending way only in the events recorded in the Bible and most specifically in the events of Jesus' life, death, and resurrection. The religion built upon this narrow view of the Spirit's work thus has objectified certain spiritual experiences, such as the life of Jesus, and has maintained that the kind of spiritual power contained in such events can never be repeated or transcended. Western religion has thus largely manifested itself through the synagogue and the church and established itself on the basis of authoritative rituals, Scriptures, and unquestioned doctrinal symbols. Against the claim of the narrow or orthodox vision of the Spirit's work stands the wider, more philosophical faith of the liberal theologians and the philosophers of history. This wider vision of the work of the Spirit is seen especially in the philosophy of Hegel, the very recent philosophy of Karl Jaspers,[11] and the systematic theology of Paul Tillich. Tillich's theology answers the question of where the Spirit is manifested by saying that the Divine Spirit's invasion of the human spirit does not occur in isolated individuals but in social groups. It is the group that is Spirit-bearing and thus history-making in Tillich's system. However, the manifestation of the Spirit, which is the mark of historical progress, is not done in some kind of collective experience or group decision, but actually is accomplished by the grasping of an individual by the Spirit within the group. The conditions for such a state of being grasped, however, are made possible only by that individual's participation in the life of his social group, be it tribe, nation, or church. This is the case because all the functions of the human spirit, moral self-integration, cultural self-creation, and religious self-transcendence, are conditioned by man's social context. Man is constituted as man by the context of social interrelations which is the life of a historical group.

The Spiritual Presence is manifested in all history, but history itself is not the manifestation of the Spiritual Presence. There are marks by which the Spiritual Presence indicates its presence in a group: (1) the presence of symbols (religious or philosophical) through which the group expresses its openness to the Spirit's impact, and (2) the rise of personalities and movements that fight against the universal tragedy of the unavoidable profanization and demonization of these religious symbols.[12]

Tillich cites the Old Testament history of Israel and Judah as a familiar example of the struggle of the prophets against the profanization of Yahweh religion and the transformation of the group under the Spiritual Presence manifest in them. However, Tillich declares that "mankind is never left alone," [13] for the Divine Spirit breaks into all history in revelatory experiences that have saving and transforming character. There is always new being in history although only in a fragmentary sense, since the participation in the transcendent unity of unambiguous life is always partial, never complete. Tillich here quotes Paul, who speaks of the anticipation of the possession of the Spirit, for the fulfillment of transcendent union is an eschatological concept. However, even these fragmentary participations are salvatory and healing, for even such a fragment points unambiguously to the Divine Power it represents. Throughout history the new being does conquer — at least partially — the ambiguities of life in time and space.

Tillich's Concept of the Church

The most basic expression of Tillich's appreciative evaluation of the church is his declaration concerning the Christhead of the Christ: "The Christ would not be the Christ without those who receive him as the Christ." [14] This is, perhaps, the highest view of the theological importance of the church ever held by a theologian. The church is not simply helpful (or beneficial, in older language, part of the *bene esse*) to God's activities, but it is necessary (part of the very being or *esse*) to God's salvatory actions through the Christ. The Athanasian Creed had always said " God and man make one Christ," but it remained for Tillich to develop the full implications of that confession. Tillich, although more an apologetic than a kerygmatic or church theologian (like Karl Barth), actually has the highest possible conception of the church — higher even than the Roman Catholic view which sees Peter and " his successors " as the vicars of Christ but not as his confirmers and cocreators. Despite this, Tillich rarely if ever used the word " church " in his writings. He explained this phenomenon in the following words: " We do not use the word ' Church ' for the Spiritual Community, because this word has been used, of necessity, in the frame of the ambiguities of religion. At this point we speak instead of that which is able to conquer the ambiguities of religion — the New Being." [15] Tillich goes on to declare that the terms " body of Christ " or " spiritual community " better express the new life created by the Spirit — and hence are the terms he prefers to use in discussing the new community created by the impact of the Divine Spirit upon the lives of men and the structures of society.[16]

Tillich is especially clear in pointing out that the spiritual community is always only fragmentarily present. Never is the new humanity present in its fullness. The full manifestation of the spiritual community (i.e., the Kingdom of God) is something that takes place "beyond history." There are to be no utopias in the life of historical mankind.

Because the spiritual community is at best fragmentary (although unambiguous, or saving, in that one has union with God today in a fragmentary moment or "eternal now"), the spiritual community is "hidden" or invisible — seen by the eyes of faith alone. This invisible spiritual community is as invisible as the Spiritual Presence is invisible, and as self-revealing as the Spirit is self-revealing, through its effects — the development of faith, hope, and love in human beings. There is between the invisible spiritual community and the visible churches a dialectical relationship of identity and nonidentity. The invisible community created by the Spiritual Presence overlaps the visible boundaries of the actually existing churches, but does not include everyone (and everything) within those churches, nor does it stop with their boundaries.

The idea of the overlapping quality of the spiritual community is simultaneously one of the most traditional ideas and one of the most liberal and creative concepts in Tillich's theology. The basic questions of religious men have always been, "Who, what, and where is the Divine Spirit (or Spirits)?" These questions have been asked (and are still asked) both in primitive and in sophisticated ways. Men ask: "Where in the world is the Spirit?" and "What are the signs of the Spirit's presence?" The answers have been as varied as the personalities and societies that have produced those answers, and yet the median range of these answers from the past and the present is amazing in its broad agreement. Tillich's phenomenological (i.e., descriptive) approach to theology makes full use of this consensus concerning the Spirit, and concerning the marks of the spiritual community.

The Marks of the Spirit's Presence

If there is one concept that characterizes the testimony of witch doctor and seer, philosopher and theologian, evangelist and apostle, to the marks of the Spiritual Presence, it is ecstasy. One who has been grasped by the Divine Presence is carried beyond himself; he is in a state of self-transcendence, such that his behavior and apperceptions are heightened and skewed in strange new ways. To the ancient Greeks, such an ecstatic experience was equivalent to madness. To be transcendent over one's self, one's space and time, was to be "beside oneself." In this state men prophesied and the priestess of the Delphic oracle gave wise (or gnomic) utterances that were taken as riddles from the gods. Among the ancient Hebrews the distinction between the soothsayer or seer who pretended to (or truly believed he could) predict the future and the prophet of Yahweh was at first ill-defined. Men were caught by catatonic trances. They saw visions and dreamed dreams, like Saul when he was chosen king of Israel (I Sam. 10:10-13), or like the glorious pagan, Socrates, who, Plato tells us, stood on one foot through one long day and night communing with the demonic voice of his god (*Symposium,* 220, b).

Later, the Hebrew (i.e., Old Testament and New Testament) conception of what constituted a Spirit-bearing or prophetic personality was subtly shifted from the physically guaranteed basis of genuineness gained from epilepticlike conditions and trances to the ethical and social powers of the prophet's utterances. The mark of the prophet who spoke of God, saying, not "This I speak," but "Thus saith the Lord," became the degree of the prophet's transcendence over earthly loyalties such as patriotism (Jeremiah) and even devotion to the accepted religion (Amos 4:4-13; Jer. 7:3-34). It was the false prophet who promised peace to the people, prosperity and victory to the king and army, and pronounced God's blessings on the priesthood and cultus. The mark of the true prophet was his utter disdain and rejection of the patriotic, social, and cultic ideals of the Hebrew people! Never has a religion held a higher view of the Spiritual Presence or been more open to the movements of God.

Jesus was a prophet in the sense that Jeremiah, Amos, and Hosea were, for he too spoke for God against people, temple, and priest. In him self-transcendence came to a pinnacle. He bore the Spirit in its fullness — a fact symbolized in the Gospels by the descent of the Spirit in the form of a dove on Jesus at his baptism (Matt. 3:16-17).

In Tillich's theological system the essence of the church is its bearing of the Spirit. Of course, an organization does not bear anything; only the people who make up an organization are capable of bearing anything. While it is true that in Tillich's thought history is made by Spirit-bearing groups, it is nevertheless the case that the Spirit is borne within these groups by Spirit-filled individuals. The same is true of the church, for the church, an ambiguous and very mixed community or group, does bear the Spirit. It does so, however, precisely through the individuals within it who have been grasped by the Divine Spirit and who therefore partially manifest the Spirit in an unambiguous fashion within the ambiguities and turmoil of history.

Tillich speaks of five elements that characterize the spiritual community.[17] He derives these five elements from a symbolic reading of the Pentecost account in The Acts.[18] The first element Tillich discusses is the ecstatic, the element of self-transcendence, of being driven beyond one's natural powers to new insights and new ways of courageous living.

The second element Tillich distinguishes in the Pentecost account is the creation of faith in Jesus as the Christ who is confessed to be the bearer of the new being, or of a new relationship to God. The act of being grasped by the Divine Spirit brings the members of the spiritual community into a

new relationship with Jesus and enables them to retain faith
in him even though he was put to death on the cross. Tillich
declares that without such faith there is no spiritual community.[19]

The third element that characterizes the spiritual community is the inception in the members of the community of a
love that expresses itself in service toward others. Again Tillich declares that apart from such self-giving love there is no
spiritual community.[20]

The fourth element in the creation of the spiritual community by the descent of the Spirit is the creation of unity. The
Pentecost story shows particularly clearly that faith in the
bearer of the new being made a brotherhood out of individuals from many different nations, races, and traditions. Thus we
cannot call any group a part of the spiritual community if it
lacks this unity and if it does not confess that one of its major aims is the creation of brotherhood, the overcoming of differences, the destruction of all prejudices, and the ultimate reunion of all estranged men with one another and with God.[21]

The fifth element that characterizes the spiritual community
and is beautifully expressed in the Pentecost account is the
drive toward universality that is expressed in the missionary
impulse of the early disciples. Tillich declares that they felt
they must give their message to everyone "because the New
Being would not be the New Being were not mankind as a
whole and even the universe itself included in it." [22] Tillich
therefore concludes that no group can be considered part of
the spiritual community unless it is open to all individuals,
races, and groups and unless it has a drive to take them into
itself.[23]

We have discussed above the five elements that are indicators of the presence of the spiritual community in the thought
of Paul Tillich. These characteristics, which are very closely
related to the traditional characteristics of the Christian
church according to the usual development of theology — that

the church is one, holy, and catholic — are found only where the Spirit has manifested itself, according to Tillich. Just because an institution is called the church does not mean that it has any one or all of these characteristics. They may or they may not be present. Only our experience with such groups can tell us whether they truly bear the Spirit. In a real sense only a phenomenological description of the church is possible. On the other hand, these elements may be found present in individuals and groups that have no connection — that the human eye can see — with the church. There is a manifestation of the Spirit possible in every aspect and area of life.[24] Tillich speaks of this manifestation in terms of the latent and the manifest stages of the spiritual community. There is a latent (or potential) state that exists wherever men are grasped by the Spirit apart from any encounter with the central revelation, which, of course, is faith in Jesus as the Christ. The manifest stage is that which comes into being when men are grasped by the Spirit along with or after an encounter with the central revelation of Jesus as the Christ.[25]

Tillich's conception of the latent church is very important to modern Christianity in its search for new and creative ways to reform the church and to humanize society. The latent (or potential) church is not limited to the Old Testament period before the manifestation of Jesus as the Christ, nor is it to be confused with the traditional distinction between the visible and the invisible church. The latent aspect of the spiritual community is rather to be seen in groups and in individuals who are outside the bounds of the manifest church but who nevertheless are bearers of the Spirit — a Spirit-bearing that is validated by the creativity and healing nature of their lives. Tillich often identified the religious socialist movement in post-World War I Germany with a latent manifestation of the spiritual community. He also saw several of the movements within modern art as such latent bearers of the Spirit. It is possible that, today, we might consider various youth, educational, la-

bor, and other movements as latent bearers of the creating and
healing presence of the Divine Spirit. It is clear, then, that according to Tillich the spiritual community is something that is
guaranteed only by the possession of the spiritual strength that
comes from bearing the Divine Spirit. In this possession the
churches have no monopoly, for the world is more vast than
the church and God is not bound to the church. God is at work
throughout the whole world, and in this work the manifest
churches have an important role but do not have the whole
role to themselves. In a day that is examining the possibility
of a religionless Christianity and is confronted by theologies
which declare that theologians in the present and future must
oppose themselves to historical theology and to the church,
this kind of insight into the larger nature of the spiritual enterprise might be enlightening. The churches are not excluded
from the spiritual community, contrary to the declarations of
Harvey Cox and Thomas Altizer, but neither are the organizations of the secular world excluded from that spiritual community. God is at work everywhere in all times and in all
places and through all kinds of men.

The Marks of the Spiritual Community

Tillich develops his description of the marks of the spiritual
community in a very traditional fashion, maintaining that the
spiritual community in itself, as it is a partial anticipation of
the transcendent union of unambiguous life, is one, holy, and
catholic. Its unity, holiness, and universality are all expressions
of its participation in the agape — the love of the Divine Spirit.
Here as in many other areas of his development of the doctrine of the Spirit, Tillich is influenced by Paul. He develops
the term " Community of Faith " on the model of the body of
Christ and its individual members, drawn from Paul (I Cor.
12:12-31). He has in mind the Pauline confession, " Christ is
in me, and I am in Christ " (Gal. 2:20), saying of the faith of
the spiritual community: " It is faith, . . . overcoming the in-

finite gap between the infinite and the finite." [26] In his description of the spiritual community as a community of love, Tillich clearly bases his development on Paul's description of agape-love in I Cor., ch. 13.

One of the basic definitions of the church in Protestant theology is that "the Church is found wherever the Word of God is rightly preached and the Sacraments rightly administered" (Augsburg Confession, Article VII). For Paul Tillich the church is also the locus of the sacramental community and the place where the Word of God is spoken. This is the manifest church, for the latent church may not, and probably does not, have any contact with the sacraments in the narrow sense of either two or seven holy actions that are said to convey grace to the believer. Rather, the spiritual community, as it is a larger and more inclusive circle than the narrow circles that form the boundaries of the various Christian churches, and is more extensive than the area described by all of them taken together, is founded on a pan-sacramentalism in which everything that exists is seen to be capable of mediating the Spiritual Presence to individuals and groups who are open to that Presence. The spiritual community is the unity of all three functions of human life as it is characterized by the dimensions of the human spirit: religion, culture, and morality. Thus "culture is the form of religion and religion is the substance of culture." [27] In the spiritual community, taken in the broad sense, there are no religious acts or religious symbols, because the spiritual community participates in every symbol and in every act of culture and morality as the creative ground and fulfillment of those acts and symbols.

A Critique of the Sacramental Concept in Theology

The spiritual community in the narrower sense of a manifest and specifically Christ-centered group does, however, have sacraments that vary from the traditional Protestant two, the Lord's Supper and Baptism, through various high-church evaluations of confirmation, marriage, and holy orders in the Anglican Communion to the Roman Catholic Church's traditional seven sacraments. No matter what the number, the theory behind the institution of these sacraments and their year-by-year repetition remains the same. This theory is fairly simple despite the complexities erected upon its primitive basis. The sacramental theory rests upon the assumption that certain actions have been ordained, promised, or ordered by God for the reception of certain spiritual gifts that are necessary to or at least beneficial for the human spirit in its quest for union with God. In the case of the Protestant Church the smaller number of sacraments is closely tied to direct institution by Christ himself, which is fairly easy to see in the case of the Lord's Supper but is not so clear in the case of Baptism since John's Gospel distinctly reports that Jesus himself baptized no one (John 4:2). What is even more disturbing to the simplistic Protestant view is the report in John of Jesus' washing the disciples' feet and his recommendation that the disciples do likewise (John 13:1-20), which seems to give the act of foot washing a firmer Protestant sacramental basis than that of Baptism. In the case of an expanded series of sacraments which include rites that embrace the high points of human life (birth, maturity, marriage, vocation for the ministry, forgiveness of sins, and death), the basis remains the same — institution by or at least attachment to a promise of God. In the case of the Roman Catholic Church the whole record of God's dealing with his chosen people in both the Old and New Testaments is used as the basis for the sacraments, rather than the more or less artificial Protestant conception of direct institution by Christ. Underlying both Catholic and Protestant sacramental theories is the apprehension of the separation between God and man and the need of man for divine assistance. The sacraments are, in the words so familiar to all, " visible signs of an invisible grace."

There is no doubt that the manifest church, the spiritual

community as it appears in its organized form, has need of
and has theological warrant for its sacraments. However, the
movement toward an opening of the church to the world in
recent times indicates that the churches need to overcome the
sharp distinction between the latent and manifest forms of the
spiritual community, and to reemphasize the pan-sacramental
basis of the unique sacraments that constitute the manifest
church. In a very real sense this is the most constructive theological way that the present-day churches can rise to the challenge of the leaders of the World Council of Churches, who
are saying that we should take Bonhoeffer's call for a church
in the world seriously, and form the agenda of the church
around the agenda of the world.

It is necessary to be very clear that the unity of religion with
culture and morality, which is included in the spiritual community, is at best a fragmentary and limited unity. Within the
spiritual community, in individuals who bear the Spirit, such
a unity is unambiguous and real, but it is fragmentary and
partial, for it takes place in finite individuals under the limitations of space and time. We cannot believe that the Kingdom
of God has come or is coming in a completely realized way
within the spiritual community, or the church either narrowly
or widely understood, within human history. To believe that
such a unity could be perfectly achieved is either to fall into
perfectionism and moralism or to lose ourselves in utopianism.
The full and unambiguous unity of religion, culture, and
morality is something that is open only to faith while history
endures, and is the object of faith above and beyond human
history.

The Function of Reformation in the Spiritual Community

Tillich speaks of three functions of the spiritual community
when it expresses itself through a church. These are the functions of (1) constitution, (2) expansion, and (3) construction.[28]

The functions of constitution stand under a polar tension of
tradition and reformation. In this function the church struggles to establish itself through the development of tradition
and theology, and, at the same time, through continual self-
reformation, to criticize and purify its theological and practical basis.

The functions of expansion stand under the polarity of ver-
ity (truth to its message) and adaptation (of the message to
the needs of the times) and relate to the missionary impulse
of the church which seeks to evangelize the whole world.

The functions of construction relate to the actualization of
the spiritual community within the life of the churches.[29]
Through this function we are concerned with the functions of
constitution and with the tension that has always existed
within the church between tradition and reformation. Without
tradition there would be no ongoing life or sense of identity
within the church. There is no option as to whether or not to
observe tradition; there is only the question as to which traditions will be observed, and how and why. However, tradition, like an individual's past life experiences, may be detri-
mental as well as beneficial. It is at this point that the continuing drive toward reformation enters in. Reformation is the
critical and continual reassessment of the traditions of the
church. The impulse to reform the church is the healthy desire
of creative and sensitive men and women who wish to " open
windows " and drop items of tradition that are lifeless and
unhelpful.

The danger that the church encounters in its natural dependence upon tradition, Tillich names demonic *hybris,* or
pride. The danger of the emphasis on reformation is that it
may degenerate into destructive criticism. In his well-bal-
anced fashion, Tillich holds that both tradition and reformation are necessary to the life of the spiritual community. However, it is important that we understand Tillich's views on the
possibly destructive nature of the reformation impulse, since

we are concerned here with calling for a new reformation of the Christian church.

Tillich also declares that the reformation impulse has a dual connotation. The first, as a historical referent to the events of the sixteenth century; and the second, to the permanent activity of the Spirit's fight against the ambiguity of religion in every era. Tillich points out a very startling and yet helpful insight: that *there is no objective criterion for a movement of reformation*, not even in the Bible, since the Bible must itself be interpreted in every historical period. All the Christian has is his sense of the freedom of the Spirit and the courage that the reception of the Spirit brings, which enables him to take the risk of reforming the church over and over again. Protestantism is the embodiment, or at least it is ideally so, of the willingness to take the risk of reformation although it may mean the destruction of particular churches. The Protestant Christian can take this risk because of his belief that the spiritual community itself cannot be destroyed.[30]

Tillich asks the question of how far the drive toward reformation can go without going so far that the church is destroyed through destructive criticism. He raises this question which is of such importance to us because, again, by its nature there can be no absolute answer to it. The fact that all criticism is not constructive and that some criticism could destroy necessary elements in the spiritual community is often used by church authorities to suppress all criticism. Here equal and opposite errors cancel one another out. The two movements toward tradition and toward reformation can never be allowed to rest in any arrangement except one of tension. The spiritual community is able to live with this tension, and any promotion of one movement over the other would destroy the spiritual basis of the church.

In the next chapter we will be concerned to investigate the radical movement toward reformation in the second half of the twentieth century. Many voices are calling for a new reformation and some are saying that such a period of renewal has already begun. In our study we will be concerned to ask, " Where in the church as we know it today is that sense of the ambiguity of the Spirit's bearers, and that allegiance to humble responsibility for one another that has always been the mark of those drawn by Christ into the spiritual community? " It is not clear that such humility and responsibility are the possessions either of those who defend the church as it is or of those who attack the church and call for renewal. It is our task to remind both sides that a church without a reformation is spiritually dead, but a reformation without an allegiance to the traditions of the church is but an unconscious reaction against forces one does not understand.

Chapter V
The New Reformation of the Twentieth Century

For over thirty years religiously-oriented men and women have been describing the end of the common era in Western religious life that began in the sixteenth century. Paul Tillich wanted to entitle his series of essays (in 1937) "The End of the Protestant Era?" but the publisher narrowed the title down to *The Protestant Era*.[1] In more recent years, Gabriel Vahanian[2] has popularized what many intellectuals have been saying for decades — that this is the end of the Christian era. It is common to speak of our time as a post-Christian one. Bishop John A. T. Robinson, in his provocative little book *The New Reformation?*[3], suggests that the historical period which worked out the problems of the "old Reformation" has now come to an end. Robinson's suggestions — with the evidence he presents — carry a lot of weight, for he also observes that the Roman Catholic Counter Reformation is over too. Paul van Buren[4] and Harvey Cox[5] have written persuasively that the era of the separation of the sacred and the secular is over — which, of course, they see as a beneficial thing, a judgment they share with Thomas J. J. Altizer.[6] Altizer and his associate, William Hamilton,[7] go even farther to declare that this is the era of the death of God.

In a very serious and concerned way Paul Tillich in his last years, joined by the famous historian of religion Mircea Eliade, explored the possibility that we are now living in a period when the distinctions between the Christian and non-Christian religions have broken down.[8]

The major question that must be asked about these declarations is: Does coming to the end of one era guarantee that we are at the beginning of another? It is not clear that we are — except in the minds of those who in their faith, hope, and love are longing for such a new reformation. What are the positive signs, if any, that a new reformation is beginning?

The Underground Church

As we have previously mentioned, the real problem faced by the Christian church today is that of rapid change — technological, social, economic, philosophical (or ideological), and political. There is no doubt that such changes, mounting up to *change* as a new order of being, have been going on for many years. The doubt — on the part of churchmen — enters when one attempts to evaluate the meaning of such changes. Briefly put, the conservative elements within the church (which are statistically in the majority) see these changes as threatening to the church and its mission, while the liberal elements welcome (or at least tolerate) such change. The rapidly growing radical movement that cuts across all denominational lines (and that is coming to constitute a kind of "underground church") advocates and celebrates the flux of change, to the discomfort of many liberals as well as of all conservatives.

The concept of the "underground church" is both new and old — like most religious concepts and phenomena. It is a new term, borrowed from the artistic and literary "underground." It is, however, a conscious Americanization of Bonhoeffer's older descriptive term "religionless Christianity." [9] The actual coining of the neologism, or new term, was done by Malcolm Boyd, who based his ideas on Bonhoeffer, John A. T. Robinson, and Bishop James A. Pike. Pike's advocacy of "traveling light" theologically, of reforming the institutional church (by accepting government taxation, etc.[10]), and his serious concern

for a mature and sensitive Christian involvement in democratic institutions is certainly part of the readily accepted man-
ifesto of the unorganized community of common concern that
we may well call " the underground church." [11]

Bishop Robinson's decisive inquiry, " Can the Christian
church be the carrier of new life for the new age? " [12] is the
question and the problem addressed by those who may be
counted as part of the underground church. The radicals have
answered this question with a " No " and a " Yes." " No," the
church as it now exists cannot serve as such a bearer of the
Spirit, and the Spirit can be brought to bear on our cultural
problems only in spite of, and perhaps outside, the present institutional church with its " church theology." But, all radical
Christians have agreed (on the basis of different analyses, of
course) that " Yes," the Christian church can and must be the
bearer of new life through the Spirit to the new age in which
we live.

The chief sign of the presence of a new reformation already
begun and waiting for implementation is the finding of one
another by the many discontented, radical, and concerned persons throughout the fabric of the various Protestant churches
and also within the Roman Catholic communion (not to men-
tion the finding of sensitive Jews, humanists, and socialists by
such church members). The attractive power of great human
problems and social issues has brought men and women from
every denomination into contact with one another and fostered
a brotherhood among those who find themselves against the
church for the sake of the church. Indeed, the major evidence
for the underground (and not so hidden) stirrings of a new
reformation is to be found in the reforms already brought into
being in American society by the cooperative work of this minority group within the churches. The order of the day has
been God-world-church in the spirit of Bishop Robinson's call
for a new reformation. Once socially sensitive men have broken the power of segregation in society, they must go on to

break its power in the church — a task that they have so far not completed. For example, in the summer of 1967, one church conference of Methodists in South Carolina voted against segregation in the church, while another conference, held at the same time in a different South Carolina city, voted to retain segregation. The end of this social and theological problem is not yet in sight.

There are many other movements besides civil rights that have brought the underground churchmen together. Opposition to the radically conservative policies of many Republican office seekers in 1964 brought the liberals and radicals together in a solid front. The various peace movements stirred to hectic activity by the war policies of the present Democratic Administration have perhaps done more to identify the genuinely radical within the church than did civil rights. Unfortunately, this aspect of the new reformation, the growth of Christian political responsibility expressed in various degrees of pacifism, has drained away so much of the concern and support of the radicals for civil rights (and disillusioned so many "establishment" liberals) that the civil rights movement is all but dead in many parts of the South. However, this may really be more evidence that the new reformation is only just beginning. It is the dawn of the new movement whose basic question is about one's responsibility to man instead of about God.[13] There *is* a new reformation, although it remains to be seen just what forms and structure such a reformation will take.

Two Basic Attitudes Toward Reformation

All views of the reformation of the church reflect one or another basic attitude toward the meaning of the historic Reformation of the sixteenth century. We may divide the chief Protestant views of the Reformation into two camps: the static and the dynamic.

The Static View. For most of the more than four hundred

and fifty years since Luther nailed his Ninety-five Theses to the Castle Church door in Wittenberg, Lutherans — following the formulations of the Book of Concord [14] and the seventeenth-century orthodox (or "scholastic") Lutheran theologians — defended and proclaimed a rather closed or static conception of the Reformation. The theological thinkers of this static camp, made up of a large part of the clergy and members of the various Lutheran churches, consider that the major job of the reformation of the church was accomplished by Luther and his followers during the period 1517 to 1600 for once and for all. Not all Lutherans — who are the largest body of Protestants, numbering over seventy million members — are committed to this view, but a good many seem to be. For these conservative Lutherans, who are best seen in the creedal position of The Lutheran Church — Missouri Synod, the task of Protestants following the time of the historic Reformation is to make good on the reforms begun then.

The Lutheran or "static" view of the reformation of the church was never the full story, however, or even the most important part of the story. From the beginnings of the sixteenth-century Reformation many other men of a more radical and dynamic frame of mind were at work on the problem of reforming the church. From the first movement of Luther to enter the reforming struggle the disagreements between various kinds of reformers began. First Luther and the humanist Erasmus broke with each other. Eventually their early sympathy turned to rancorous quarreling. Luther also clashed with Andreas Carlstadt, a fellow professor at the University of Wittenberg who championed a "Radical Reformation" that would have removed music, beauty, statuary, and almost every vestige of culture from the Reformed Church. Eventually the (old) Radical Reformation came about through the efforts of utopian fanatics like Thomas Münzer, and the work of spiritualistic pietists like Menno Simons.[15] The work of the Anabaptists or rebaptizers, as they were called, soon found refuge — and flowered — among the tolerant Dutch. From Holland the ideas of the Radical Reformers crossed the channel to England and prepared the way for the delayed Anglican reformation and the more far-reaching Methodist movement— much later — which brought the main ideas of the Continental Reformers into the life of the average citizen of Great Britain.

No one could expect that the Reformation of the sixteenth century would display a monolithic unity. Indeed the church out of which the various Protestant congregations and churches emerged, the medieval Roman Catholic Church, was itself not the seamless unity historians sometimes tend to make it. It was to be expected that once the chief bond of unity in the church, the papacy, was rejected, the organizations established by the revolting Christians would display more and more individual-istic and sectarian tendencies.

The historical factors that made a reformation of the church possible in the sixteenth century were also diverse and in some instances contradictory to each other. Among these factors we may note the emergence of the modern concept of national states in Great Britain, France, Spain, Portugal, and parts of Italy. The growth of strong kings, the expansion of Western man to the New World and to Africa and Asia, and the desire to keep some of the church taxes within the country where they were collected, all contributed to the desire for church reform. In fact, without the background of the inner struggle for control of the national organizations of the Roman Catholic Church on the part of the rising monarchs and the papacy, no reformation would have been possible.

The Reformation itself occurred as a movement within a larger historical movement known as the Renaissance. This re-vival of the ancient Greek and Latin learning began in the fifteenth century and continued throughout the sixteenth, be-coming fused with the growth of interest in natural science and the exploration and exploitation of the physical world to pro-duce the kind of world outlook that has characterized the West until this day.

Only within these larger historical events and forces did the spiritual experiences and the moral outrage of the Christian church members, who later became Protestants or reforming Catholics, become possible. Martin Luther was not born into a vacuum, nor was he the only priest or layman who came to conclude that the church must be cleansed and updated. In fact, Luther was not the first to call for reform, nor was he the last.

The static conception of church reformation which came to be identified with the position of Luther was challenged from the very beginning of the attempts of Luther to institutionalize the insights and beliefs that led him to break with the Roman Catholic Church. In particular, Luther's decision to encourage the local secular rulers to govern the churches in their realms after the authority of Rome had broken down, along with Luther's identification of the rule of these princes with the divinely given power of the sword — and his consequent condemnation of any call for political reform — lost him the support of thousands of persons who formerly sympathized with him.

First, he alienated the "Puritan" elements within the German Reformation that wished to purge all the art and music that played such a large part in traditional worship. Luther was horrified at this program and reprimanded his fellow professor, Andreas Carlstadt, who had led the mob that was destroying the icons and statues in the former Roman Catholic churches of Wittenberg. On March 6, 1522, Luther began a series of sermons that emphasized the conservative aspects of his view of the Reformation. This reactionary action cut Luther off from many Germans and Swiss, and in a sense determined that a majority of those churches which would eventually be formed on the basis of the Reformation would differ from him and his immediate followers in respect to liturgy and custom.

Secondly, Luther's encouragement of the princes to take charge of the ecclesiastical properties and to exercise oversight of the congregations within their territories alienated all those who rightfully saw in the Reformation an outbreak of the repressed desires of the common people for economic and political reforms. When the Peasants' Revolt of 1524–1526 broke out, Luther was aghast. These revolutionaries bound themselves together in covenants and demanded the dismissal of clergymen who resided outside their parishes and the right to call their own pastors. These covenanters first looked to Luther for support, seeing in his emphasis on the freedom of the Christian a model for the human freedom they wished. Among the benefits they desired were land reform and a more equitable tax. It was the movement of the common man, its symbol being the *Bundschuh,* or the peasant's shoe. However, the courageous doctor who faced the princes and bishops could not face what he saw as the breakdown of law and order, and thus Luther blasted the peasants' military action in a tract that can only be described as reactionary and excessively cruel. This tract is entitled "Against the Robbing and Murdering Hordes of Peasants." [16] Luther denounced the demands of the peasants for land reforms and implied that Christ was a stronger lawgiver than Moses, for Christ, according to Luther, bound men under the emperor and the law of this world. This doctrine of two separate kingdoms, both ordained of God, became stuck fast in the Lutheran way of looking at things and was to have fateful consequences in the next four hundred and fifty years of Christian history. It was one of the more important factors in the preservation of a static outlook on the reformation of the church.

Thirdly, Luther alienated the humanists and other evangelically-oriented Catholics in his dispute with Erasmus. At first, Luther and Erasmus were sympathetic with each other, but before long the basic incompatibility of Luther's Augustinian pessimism about human nature and Erasmus' optimistic belief in the improvability of man brought them to a rather crude break. Paradoxically, it was Erasmus' conservatism, his moderation which abhorred schism and wanted a peaceful moral cleansing of the church, which ensured the separation of the humanistic attempts at reformation from Luther's separate movement for reform.

Fourthly, Luther cut himself off from the more radical reformers in terms of the theology of the sacraments. The Anabaptists, who denied infant baptism, were alienated from Luther both by his rejection of the Peasants' Revolt in which most of them were implicated and by his insistence on the retention of infant baptism. Luther called all those who diverged from him, particularly those who preached a return to some kind of primitive Christianity, *Schwärmer*, or fanatics. He especially had to contend with the teachings of Thomas Münzer, who was not only an Anabaptist but a kind of spiritualist who preached a primitive communism and encouraged the Peasants' Revolt. It is hard to tell whether Luther was more offended by the theological or the political opinions of the Radical Reformers.

Luther also cut himself off from the more stable but also puritanical reformers of Switzerland and South Germany. He refused to agree to a relatively mild compromise on his high theological evaluation of the Eucharist with Zwingli and the reforming pastors of Strassburg. He also rejected the mediating position of the Swiss Reformers such as Bucer. An attempt was made by a political leader, Philip of Hesse, to bring Luther and Zwingli to an agreement that would permit the various reforming congregations to stand together against the Catholics.[17] Luther refused to come to an agreement with the Reformed wing, however, and thereafter the Reformation developed (even on its conservative side) in two wings.

The Dynamic View. Church history is somewhat comforting in that it tells us that the dynamic concept of reformation won the day in areas where the majority of Protestants would be made. The old Radical Reformers, the Swiss Reformers (Zwingli and Bucer), and the great, gray figure of Protestant systematic theology, John Calvin, all accepted a dynamic con-

cept of the reformation of the church. Later John Knox, the
English Reformers, and John Wesley were to be dynamic in
their approach. It is through these founders of the Baptist,
Methodist, Anglican, and Presbyterian communions that the
dynamic view of reformation was to become a significant part
of the life of the Anglo-Saxon world. It was through these communions, rather than through the millions of German Lutheran
immigrants, that the dynamic view of reformation was to enter
into the culture of the United States of America.

The non-Lutheran Reformed churches in Germany, Switzerland, France, Scotland, and Britain all affirmed more dynamic
conceptions of the Reformation than the Lutherans, a fact that
is concretized in the wide variation of church practices, poli-
ties, and liturgies in the Reformed groups. However, even the
Reformed dynamic concept of reformation was strictly limited,
which is illustrated by the emphasis of one group (the Presbyterian) on one kind of church polity as the ideal type for Christian churches, and the rather standardized Puritan (and anti-
artistic) liturgical practices that came into being in the Reformed world. The reformation of the church was surely less
dynamically understood than it might have been when one
form of church government came to be stressed to the exclusion
of others and when "high" liturgical services became suspect
as non-Reformed. In a much more basic way the theological
doctrine of predestination and the extremely narrow (or "holiness") view of Christian morality as it developed at Geneva
under Calvin were definitely high walls set around the dynamic view of churchly reformation. The fact that Calvinists
as well as Lutherans and Catholics persecuted unto death Anabaptists and Unitarians shows that even in the Reformed wing
of Protestantism the tension between static and dynamic concepts often broke down in favor of a static (or narrow) view.
These historical phenomena explain the series of later reforma-
tions that took place on the territory of the Reformed churches,
e.g., the "Covenanters" (or Associate Reformed Presbyterians

of today) in Scotland, and much later the great Methodist revival in Great Britain.

The great theological exponent of the dynamic concept of church reformation was a Reformed pastor and scholar, however. This was Friedrich Daniel Ernst Schleiermacher (1768–1834), whose famous — and sincere — theological slogan and program was " The Reformation must continue." Schleiermacher recast Protestant theology in a post-Kantian, subjectivistic mold, intending to update the teaching of the church and make it able to attract its "cultural despisers." [18] With Schleiermacher we may leave the historical investigation of the dynamic concept of reformation, for, as he is the first modern systematic theologian, all later theologians (except for the continuingly orthodox Lutherans and conservative Protestants) were to be affected by him. With Schleiermacher modern theology has arrived, and the road to Ritschl, Harnack, and Herrmann — which ends with Paul Tillich — has already begun.

The Revival of the Dynamic Concept of Reformation

The tensions and the struggles that have marked the emergence of the Christian churches into international prominence by virtue of the increasing social and political awareness of Christian thinkers and leaders make it clear that Christianity is not what it was a century ago, nor is it what seems to be demanded by the conditions of the modern era. I have discussed this turmoil elsewhere under the theme of a great divorce between Western man's mind and spirit.[19] The rise of modern critical scholarship made the static conception of reformation and the rationalistic orthodoxy that developed both in Lutheranism and in Calvinism (as well as in Catholicism) utterly irrelevant to the problems faced by religious men in a century of total war. In an ever-mounting wave the various programs and streams of theological thinking that developed in response to the rise of science, to the brutality of modern industrial life and world war, and to the increasing sensitivity of religious people to the suffering of humanity for whose alleviation their orthodox theology offered only panaceas and not remedies, crested and crashed into nothingness.

It became increasingly clear that the church itself must be cleansed and reunited if anything were to be done to make Christianity a resource for the spiritual development of man. Several major paths were developed, each of which sought in its own way to revive the Christian church and to drag it screaming and struggling into the modern world. One of these major paths was the development of liberal theology which gradually supplanted the fundamentalism that had developed on the basis of the older orthodoxy. However, this liberal theology which sought in some of its forms to substitute an enlightened social awareness for theological substance, and in others to recover the facts about the historical Jesus, finally came to reveal itself to be almost as shallow a set of responses to modern man's needs as was the fundamentalism that opposed it.[20] Another of the major paths taken in the twentieth century, and one that has borne a good deal of fruit, has been the ecumenical movement. Beginning early in the century, many Christian groups in the United States began to draw closer together in national organizations designed to increase the social awareness and political impact of the Protestant churches. These developments culminated in the formation of the Federal Council of Churches, which later became the National Council of Churches. Eventually these new organizations made international contacts through the World's Young Men's Christian Association and the International Missionary Council and then finally became part of the World Conference on Faith and Order and the Universal Christian Council for Life and Work. Under the leadership of John R. Mott, J. H. Oldham, Charles H. Brent, William Temple, and Nathan Söderblom, these various international Christian groups became increasingly active, and in 1938, the World Conference on Faith and Order and the Universal Christian Council for

Life and Work merged to form the World Council of Churches at a meeting in Utrecht. World War II delayed the further development of the World Council of Churches, but in 1948, at a large assembly held in Amsterdam, Holland, the World Council was officially constituted. Over one hundred Protestant and Orthodox churches joined, and by 1954 the number had increased to one hundred sixty church bodies. In 1967, the World Council of Churches consisted of nearly two hundred churches in all parts of the world. In 1961, the World Council of Churches was strengthened by a merger with the International Missionary Council, which has made it the chief instrument of unified Christian work among those Christians who do not accept the authority of the Church of Rome.

The New Reformation Is Not the Ecumenical Movement

The ecumenical movement is undoubtedly one of the most important historical phenomena of the twentieth century, as it has drawn the entire non-Catholic world closer together than it has ever been in history. In point of fact we cannot speak of the reunion of the church, for the unity of this large segment of Christianity must be seen as a historically unique accomplishment. The Protestant churches were never one; thus the cooperation they have enjoyed with each other in the National Council and the World Council of Churches is new. The Orthodox churches never before enjoyed the cooperation they now have with each other in these same councils. In these new agencies Protestants and Eastern Catholics have moved closer together, which is healthful for both traditions. And as an overplus of value, the World Council of Churches cooperation has attracted the interest of the Roman Catholic Church, so that both in America and throughout the world relations are warmer and more useful between the Church of Rome and the other churches than in any period of history. Examples of this new friendship are the inviting of Orthodox and Protestant observers to Vatican Councils I and II, and the visits of the pope to Palestine, the United States, India, and Turkey. The example of the cooperation of other Christians with one another, reflecting as it does the necessity for Christians to work together in times of challenge to Christendom, has also contributed to closer relationships between the pope and the Ecumenical patriarch of the Eastern Orthodox Church.

The one great drawback of the ecumenical movement which apparently disqualifies it for identification as *the* reformation of the twentieth century is that inherent in its very being is the necessity for compromise and for the minimization of differences between various communions for the sake of continued cooperation. This has brought about a bland, relatively colorless ecumenical theology that is entirely Biblical, but hardly more than that. The neo-orthodox theology of Reinhold Niebuhr rather than the philosophical theology of Tillich (or of William Ernest Hocking) or the radical theology of someone concerned to meet the problems of the modern world with a reconstruction of religion has been chosen for development by the hundreds of intelligent ministers and laymen who have devoted their lives to the ecumenical movement. It is this theological blandness which has alienated the conservatives on the one hand and the radicals on the other from this good-but-not-good-enough movement toward the reunion of the churches.

Perhaps the most serious criticism of the ecumenical movement, from the standpoint of its failure to be the one great movement of reformation in the church, is its necessary emphasis on organization-building. It has stressed the building up of new structures and agencies and has fostered the coming into being of church mergers as a legitimate consequence of its basic thrust. However, as necessary as this work is, it has taken the energy needed for a radical reform of the church and dissipated it in a new and grander program of organization-tending.

In Chapter II we discussed the failure of neo-orthodoxy as a theological movement, the new conservatism as an evangelistic movement, the right wing as a kind of patriotic reformation movement, and the neoliberal civil rights movement; therefore we will not repeat our comments here. We reiterate, however, that none of these attempts at the reformation of the American Church has worked and each is somewhat in a state of decline. If there is to be a new reformation in America, that reformation movement can only be seen as an outgrowth of the continuing understanding of the radicals from the sixteenth century until now that the reformation is a dynamic thing, an ever-changing thing, which must grow out of the needs of men where they are in the midst of their suffering and confusion. As little as it may seem to be mature, or even serious, the most promising of movements that are now calling for reform is the often confused but never unconcerned group of young and stridently radical voices that are gathered together under the catchphrase of the "new" or "radical theology."

The Radical Theology as a New or Radical Reformation Movement

The radical theology has been weakened in its thrust as a serious call for the reformation of the church by the overuse of its greatest strength, its news value. As someone has remarked, a minister who proclaims that God is alive will attract little attention, since this statement is implied or explicit in most Sunday sermons, but a minister or religion teacher who declares that God is dead has become newsworthy. At least this was the case for the first year or two of the "God is dead" excitement, for, like famines in India, earthquakes in Turkey, casualty lists from Vietnam, and reports of riots from the cities, even the enormity of the proclamation of the death of the Divine soon becomes commonplace news. Man, particularly massmedia man, is so sophisticated or so insensitive (or a combination of both) that the kinds of horrors we have described soon lose their ability to shock and so become part of the furniture of everyday life.

The radical theology's greatest strength during its first phase was its ability to attract the mass media and to become known throughout the world by television and magazine. As in the case of many other movements and institutions, this strongest point has paradoxically become its weakness. Many theologians and churchmen simply cannot credit the bearers of this shocking movement with a serious reforming interest. Perhaps some of the members of the school do not have such an interest, but it seems clear that Thomas Altizer does share a hope for the reform of Christendom — a hope and a concern that is the most attractive part of his proclamation. The most recent evidence of this concern is his article "Catholic Theology and the Death of God." [21] Many, if not all, of the younger theologians and ministers who have responded warmly to the new theology are attracted by just this reforming interest.

The twin foci of the demand for a new reformation by the radicals seem to be the secular city on the one side and the death of God on the other. Between these two poles, the new theology calls for the Christianization of mankind through the full humanization of every human being by means of radical, social change. It is a reformation that is based on a metaphysic that recognizes no world but this and no problems for man but the problems that afflict his body with disease, his mind with ignorance, his life with violence, his cities with cruelty, and his world with war. It is a humanistic philosophy, which, however, has the human Jesus as its model and not some abstraction called man, not even the shopworn abstraction called "modern man" which every theologian brings out and confronts with his conception of an up-to-date gospel. It is a theology of reformation that speaks confidently even while God is silent, for it recognizes that God has always been silent. Only man's unique reaction to and assessment of God's silence in the mid-twentieth century is new. It raises a loud voice in the name of the human Jesus and the human beings who suffer *now* from injustice, and waits for God to speak, if and when he will.

Samuel Beckett wrote of man's reaction to the silence of God in *Waiting for Godot* [22] during the opening years of America's response to the feeling that God was dead. It is interesting to note that the two half-crazed actors in the play strike at the heart of the paradoxically religious devotion to the ideal of the Christ in the midst of the secular and irreligious feeling of desolation — for neither actor seriously expects Godot to come.

André Malraux has come closer to expressing the radically religious feeling of so many twentieth-century men, a feeling that has informed the theological development of the radical theology. In Malraux's pre-World War II novel, *Man's Fate*, there occurs a scene between two European Communists who have been involved in the unsuccessful attempt of the Shanghai workers' movement to seize control of the city. The attempt has been foiled by the betrayal of the workers on the part of the Russian Communists, the Central Committee of the Chinese Communist Party, and the Kuomintang. The two men know that they are soon to die, and one, Hemmelrich, is disgusted with himself for not having gone out to fight against the enemy sooner. He has attempted to excuse himself because of his need to protect his family. Now he accuses himself of cowardice in front of his friend, Katov. Katov listens sympathetically and in a moving expression of human sensitivity tries to convince the man that he had not really used his family as a pretext to protect himself, but that he had done precisely the human thing. Katov puts in words what many others of different nationalities and different creeds have felt in the face of the brutalities of power politics in our age.

KATOV: . . . If you believe in nothing, *especially* because you believe in nothing, you're forced to believe in the virtues of the heart when you come across them, no doubt about it. And that's what you're doing. If it hadn't been for the woman and the kid you would have gone, I know you would. Well, then?

HEMMELRICH: And as we live only for those virtues of the heart, they get the better of you. Well, if you've always got to be licked, it might as well be them. . . . But all that's absurd,

It's not a matter of being right. I can't stand the idea of having put Ch'en out, and I couldn't have stood to have kept him.

KATOV: We can only ask the comrades to do what they can. I want comrades, and not saints. No confidence in saints. . . .[23]

Something of this sentiment courses through the work of Altizer, who writes so movingly of the Christ that is seen in every human face. It is found in the best of Hamilton's writings when he speaks of Jesus as a place to be, a place beside the Negro in the civil rights movement and in the efforts to improve human life that face such opposition in our selfish society. It is found in the writings of Harvey Cox, in his assessment of the secular city when he speaks of man's deep longing to find a gracious neighbor in the midst of the impersonal forces that swirl in the city's streets. It is found in a heartbreaking way in the writings of Richard L. Rubenstein, who declares that no Jew can believe that God is not dead when he considers the enormity of the mass murders of the Jews by the Nazis. The response of these men to the silence of God is then not that of Vladimir and Estragon, to wait for God, but to affirm man. It would appear that the radical theology really begins when men reject the neat answers of traditional religion that have always painted an unseen but rosy picture of the hand of God behind the horrors of the world. These men seem to have grown tired of waiting, and it is difficult to say that there may not be some justification for their attitude.

The form, then, of the new reformation must be inferred from what the playwrights and novelists have said in metaphor and from what the radical theologians have said in prophecy and in outrage — that the full humanization of mankind can only come through the humanization of society. We cannot hope to help men if we can only help them one at a time as the pious, old and new, never weary of saying. In order to humanize man we must humanize the structures in which he lives. Thus for the radical Christians the image of Christ lies ready to hand as the picture of what the full and complete human being should and can be. This is a theology of the Christian-ization of the human race, not in the sense of the conversion of men to a set of doctrines, but through the conforming of man to the lineaments of the personality of Jesus. It is not a matter of what men do or do not believe, or of what they will and will not believe, but of the becoming Christlike of human personalities.

This is also a rejection of the "sacred remnant" idea that has prevailed in much of Christianity because of its foundation in the holy history of the Old Testament and in the little com-pany of the apostles in the New. Listen to the words of a radi-cal of an earlier time who did struggle against injustice and who paid the price of exile because of his opposition to the evils of Nazism — the poet Bertolt Brecht. As Brecht has writ-ten, we cannot try to save a few and forget the masses of men:

> Who, O wretched one, shall dare it?
> He who can no longer bear it
> Counts the blows that arm his spirit,
> Taught the time by need and sorrow,
> Strikes today and not tomorrow.
>> Everything or nothing. All of us or none.
>> One alone his lot can't better.
>> Either gun or fetter.
>> Everything or nothing. All of us or none.[24]

Brecht has here put in words what the radical theologian is saying: "Everything or nothing"; "All of us or none."

Someone has said that there are only two kinds of people in the world: the kind who make things happen and the kind who have things happen to them. For too many years the church has encouraged Christians to be content to be the kind of people to whom things happen, counseling them to accept without a struggle the conditions of the world and the positions they oc-cupy. Because Christianity has had its greatest influence among peoples who have worked out ways of living in which most people have been able to live without hunger and with some hope of seeing better days, and of receiving, even after the laws' long delays, something like justice, this position has gone relatively unchallenged. Of course, millions of men have challenged this quietism by their actions while affirming it with their lips. It has been, after all, on Christian soil that capitalism has developed, which surely is not a system built up by men satisfied with their lot. However, those who challenge the precept have been more than happy to keep up the game so that others would not challenge the position they carved out for themselves. There has almost been a silent conspiracy between the church and the men who have had the courage to make things happen that has striven to prevent the masses of men from becoming active themselves in the use of power. The new theology stands as a challenge to this accommodation of Christianity with the world. The new theologian, like the poor in the urban slums who in his frustration and outrage is burning his city around him, is crying out, " All of us or none."

In summary we may say that the new reformation for which the new Christian is calling must be active in relation to politics and society. It cannot be reactive, hoping to make the best of the crises brought on by governments and social groups, as so much of the theology of the church has been. The new reformation must be formative, having a hand in the formation of the world which is being torn down and rebuilt today. It must find the power and the persuasion to shape the structures that must come to replace the decaying cities and the self-defeating international struggles that plague us. The new theologian does not come with the message of Isaiah, " Comfort, comfort my people " (Isa. 40:1), but with the message of the wrathful God given to Jeremiah: "See, I have set you this day over nations and over kingdoms, to pluck up and to break down, to destroy and to overthrow, to build and to plant " (Jer. 1:10). The new reformation must take as seriously as Jeremiah the fourfold injunction to destroy the structures of evil, and actively carry it out before it can turn to the job of construction. In a sense the new Christianity must be a new *formation* — not a *reformation*

— for the new Christianity must take seriously its human and Biblical mandate to make things happen for the good of man. It can no longer be content to be merely reformative. The new theologian is well aware that more than human sensitivity and faithfulness to the Bible impels him in this task, for on all sides he sees other movements all too willing to form society after their own image, from the movements of violence produced by both the left and the right wings of American political extremism, to the shallowness of programs for a greater society that are framed into laws by the insensitivity of the middle class. The new theologian holds out the image of Jesus as over against the image of black power on the one side, and white supremacy on the other, and the temporizing of the great society in the middle.

It is this active spirit to do good which is the motive force behind the new and radical reformation, a spirit that is the outgrowth of mankind's modern sense of historical self-consciousness which on its basic level means that man is aware that he has made himself and thus the evil he has done he has done out of his own power. Man's sense of historicity, based on the insights that have come to him through the application of the scientific structures made possible by the concept of evolution, lays the blame for the suffering and evil in the world squarely on man. He cannot take refuge in hypotheses that speak of evil and suffering as the outgrowth of the Divine Will or as just punishment for the breaking of moral laws. Man's historicity, which is both an outgrowth of his science and a basic element in his scientific method, therefore makes the modern man feel his involvement in and responsibility for the suffering and chaos of the world.

On the basis of these insights we may say that the often decried increase in the evil of the world, so loudly proclaimed by legal officials and moralists on the right wing, is based on a misunderstanding. In fact, the rising awareness of the burden of evil that rests on man is due to the coming to consciousness

—in large masses of people —of the mental outlook we have called historical self-consciousness. This new outlook, which has a long and distinguished history among philosophers and writers in the past, has become the property of the masses of men only in the twentieth century through revolutionary propaganda, the rise of the labor movement, through the development of the mass media of communication, and, underlying all of these historical forces, through increasingly effective public education.

It is not that man is becoming more evil or that society is more violent, the new theologian says, but that man is becoming ever more sensitive to violence and evil. No more wickedness exists today than in the past; perhaps less exists, for men have overcome slavery and made advances against the conquest of ignorance and disease, but more of us are aware of more of the background of violence and exploitation that is a constant factor in the world. On this view the much-denounced moral breakdown of our time is not a sign of the decline of culture or the death of religion, but is the sign of the increasing moral sensitivity, we might say of the increasing moral commitment, of the masses of men. Man is not degenerating, but man is aware of the degeneration inherent in much of the world's social structure, and he is aware of the degeneration of some classes of men who perpetuate structures of evil that constantly provoke violence, although they may give themselves out to be the most moral of men.

We may say that the new or radical reformation which we have called a drive toward a formation of a new Christianity is a call for the Christian to become an active agent in the decisions about what the future of man will be like. This new reformation has both an inner and an outer dynamic thrust and concern. In its inner drive it aims at the full humanization of man through the full development of man's personality to the point where the attributes of Jesus become strong in him. In order to accomplish this the radical believes that all men must be freed in their external relationships and fulfilled in their educational, financial, and social dimensions. The inner drive, therefore, leads directly to the exterior thrust of the new reformation, to the drive toward full citizenship of every human member of national social orders, and the development of peaceful relationships between members of the same societies and between the larger societies and nations of men.

Many traditionally religious people will see this description of the thrust of the new reformation as confirming its worldly character, thus denouncing it as a social or economic movement in the same way that much of the ecumenical theology has been so judged and condemned. We must say that the new theology does have affinities with the ecumenical theology, particularly to the theology of Reinhold and H. Richard Niebuhr. We may also say that it has similarities to the Social Gospel movement of an earlier period of American history. But this does not mean that the older forms of theology that stressed engagement with the world or the new theology today are a kind of religiously based socialism only. The new theology, like its predecessors, is firmly based on the Gospel accounts of the figure of Jesus. It is a new piety that weaves itself about the image of that One who spoke as no other man has spoken. It is a call to radical obedience to the ethic that Jesus not so much taught as lived. It is a reaction against the decision of Schweitzer and the other older theologians who felt that Jesus' ethic was impractical for the long haul of history and suitable only for a brief period before the end of the world.

The new theology is amazingly naïve and unsophisticated in its approach to the New Testament. Arguments based on historical judgments are not allowed to blunt the point of Jesus' assertion that we should love one another. In some other respects the new theology bases its concept of reformation also on Paul, who stressed the mystical and yet organic unity of the spiritual community. This spiritual community, or body of Christ, within which each man bears the Christ (or as Altizer has said, reveals the Christ in every human face), is the real goal of the radical reformer. The radical believes that the spiritual community is already here; it needs only to be recognized and man's awareness of it deepened. This Spiritual Presence is not foreign to man but is precisely the full development of his own humanity. In brief, to be a fully developed man is to be a Christian, and to be a Christian is to be a man. This organic, spiritual unity, the radical feels, must become more and more realized in a human solidarity against all that is partial or partisan, against all that causes human misery, fear, want, and war.

What the radical reformation really desires is for every spiritually sensitive person to work for a world where:

There will be no slaves.

Where every man in every country says, " I will not fight " except against ignorance and disease, prejudice and pain through nonviolence;
There will be no wars.

Where every man says, " I will be free, have enough to eat, a good place to live, books and music for my mind and spirit, a right to worship or not as I see fit ";
There will be true freedom.

Where every man and woman says, " We will bear only those children we genuinely desire ";
There will be families.

Where everyone says, " I will not live in ignorance nor die in fear, nor suffer needless pain and deprivation in the interim between birth and death ";
Then there will be true men on the earth and we can once again discuss the problem of God.

Chapter VI
The Form of the Church of the New Reformation

IN AN EARLIER CHAPTER we discussed the social characteristics of the modern age, accepting the slogan "man come of age" from Bonhoeffer as a possible description of the second half of the twentieth century, if we understand that it is the age itself (i.e., Western mankind taken as a whole) that is come of age and not any ascertainable individual men. Our period is one that has matured in the sense of noetic maturity — a maturity of knowledge. It is an age characterized by a full development of that great nineteenth-century achievement, historical self-consciousness. I have developed my conception of this sense of historicness in another place,[1] observing that men today do not ask questions of being, but questions of development. We do not ask, "Where did we come from?" but rather, "How did we get the way we are?" This principle of noetic maturity accounts for the overall characteristics of life in our era, which is an era of general sophistication and a self-conscious awareness of evolutionary developments in which all myths (social, economic, religious, and political) are demythologized, or better, deliteralized.

Man come of age can only be Western mankind taken as a whole (including men in the Soviet-dominated Eastern European countries and in the Soviet Union itself), for every one of us now living is certainly not living in the same era. Just as the generations of men overlap one another, even so do historical eras overlap. Many older people are scandalized by developments that have taken place in the last decade because these people are not flexible enough to be reborn in the new world that has dawned with the advent of those forms of historic self-consciousness which affirm the death of God and man's ability to regulate his states of awareness through psychedelic drugs.[2] Within the population at any one time a variety of historic eras are represented dwelling side by side: eras that are perpetuated long after they come to a close in external reality through their formative influence on men and women born under the impress of forces characteristic of those eras, either because they were born when those eras were in the ascendancy or because those influences were imposed on them by their parents (or political or religious leaders), who felt that there was some sanctity about those modes of thought.

This is a complicated concept and one that may be difficult to understand, as it supposes that everyone alive at a certain moment or point in time does not really inhabit the same moment of history. It also is a discouraging concept, for it supposes that many groups of men may be unable to really speak to one another because they are the inhabitants of what amounts to different worlds, even though they may look alike, live by the same physical substances, displace space in the same way, and fruitfully interact on many levels. However, it appears to be an increasingly necessary hypothesis, because there do exist in the world of the 1960's men who believe that the last word about life was spoken two or three thousand years ago, and other men alongside them who believe that all the necessary correctives for religious ideas were worked out four hundred and fifty years ago.

Religion is not the only field that reveals such odd behavior. There are many persons in America who feel that the founding fathers included all political wisdom for all time in the Constitution and the Bill of Rights and who, therefore, resist any effort to devise more modern means of governing the country.

In Europe and Asia (especially in China) there are many who apparently believe that Karl Marx has spoken the last word on economics and political life. Everyone in the West witnesses with a kind of fascinated horror the sight of Mao Tse-tung [3] trying to drag the Chinese nation forward into the late nineteenth century. There *are* divisions among men, it would appear, but they are divisions made up by types of historic self-consciousness and not by the usual divisions attributed to nationality, race, and religion.

There have been reports by social scientists, ministers, and other concerned adults about the apparent gap between the younger generation and persons over thirty years of age. The older generation is somewhat shocked and more than a little surprised that the young people are not overjoyed by the kind of world that has been prepared for them. This is a period in Western history that, while not the Pax Romana, is still a period of relative peace and of unprecedented prosperity. Aside from the continuing turmoil between Israel and her Arab neighbors, and the endless waste of life in the Indo-Chinese War that has stretched from 1941 to the present, there is a kind of global truce between the giant powers. The war in Vietnam is highly significant as an element in the call of the young radicals for the reformation of both society and church, and yet the death rate in that struggle is but a small part of the number of Americans who are accidentally killed on national holidays and on the long weekends made possible by industrial automation.

This being the case, why is it that the present-day high school and college youth are growing ever more critical of national policies and of the moral teachings of the church? Their increased sensitivity is explainable only if we understand that they are exhibiting a new form of historic self-consciousness, one that is characterized by a political realism that has often been missing in North American life. The fact is that the present student generation is politically self-conscious in the sense

that political self-consciousness was considered a virtue by the
communists and socialists of the old left who worked so hard
in the 1930's to bring such a consciousness to the workers of
America. The old left failed, but the new left has been born
in its own time, and the parents of those who now hold such
views can only look and wonder where such mutations came
from. The young people of today, who will be the voters and
the church members (if there is a church) of a very fast coming tomorrow, see the self-seeking and the class bias in every
political program and in every evangelistic program of the
middle-class government and the middle-class church in their
moves to win the world of the alienated in the university, the
high school, and the slum.

None of the above interpretations is discredited by recent
sociological findings that the hard-core members of the new
left are the children of very liberal families.[4] We are not discussing the hard-core leadership of the new left but the
younger generation as a whole. In all events the new left is
more opposed to the so-called liberal establishment than to any
other sector of the modern American nation, so this information
merely supports our thesis.

The problematic or hard-core areas that the bearers of the
Spirit must identify with, invade, and if possible, redeem, can
be summed up under several headings. Because the study of
these problem areas lies outside the scope of our present problem, we simply introduce them here as a background for our
assessment of how the church must move to reform itself. In
the Notes we give suggestions for further reading and study
concerning each of these areas that may be consulted by the
interested reader.

The "Death of God" Theology

Despite the wishes of many theologians, both liberals and
conservatives, including the editors of *The Christian Century*,
the "death of God" theology is not dead. Many of us may wish
that it would die and go away, but apparently it will not. It

will not go away because it is symbolic of the problems and needs of our historical period in a far more important way than it is significant as a philosophical or theological movement. As I have pointed out elsewhere, the "death of God" movement is only the latest in a culture-long tradition of contrapuntal movements that have arisen in the West as correctives to the failures and prostitutions of the Western religious heritage by the orthodox establishment.[5]

Until a short time ago the radical theology was limited to a Protestant expression, but in the last year or two there has arisen a distinguished Jewish representative of this type of thought, Rabbi Richard L. Rubenstein, who is now proclaiming the message of Judaism and the death of God.[6] The unique in-
ent, Thomas J. J. Alti-
f the "death of God"
thought by writing a
gy and the Death of
hought and brings up
discussed by theolo-
significant point Altizer
we have been saying
onsciousness, and re-
al task of the church.

understanding of the
cosmos, and likewise
ntegral reality of the
then we are faced
ption of the relation
al movement of hu-
e which has at least
eilhard de Chardin.
open to the Catho-
nthropology in on-
r understanding of
ssity of natural or
theological think-

In the decades to come there undoubtedly will arise other theological novelties, and new popular figures will replace the great fallen giants like Tillich, Schweitzer, and Barth, but the problem raised by the "death of God" theologians will continue to trouble the church. The church had better learn to deal positively and constructively with this movement.

The Reaction Against the Institutional Church

The warm endorsement given the radical critiques of the contemporary Christian church in this book rests upon two basic beliefs: the first, that the reformation of the church is a never-ending task that must continue throughout history; and the second, that modern man's experience of the silence (or death) of God is the voiceless call of the Spirit for the reform of the church.

Just how does one approach the reform of the church? Perhaps there is no better method than that of testing the church against criteria it already accepts. Jesus' statement that we shall know good trees (and men) by their fruits and bad trees (and evil men) by the like sign is as good a criterion as any.

Judged by its fruits, the church must receive a mixed judgment. The church has done much good in the world, and has had an overwhelmingly salutary effect on the lives of millions of men. But its good effects have been deficient because they have been limited. Not deficient because the church has been able only fragmentarily and partially to manifest the Spirit, not deficient because the church has been able to aid only a finite (and limited) number of men, but deficient because there have been limitations laid on the gospel by the church, limitations not inherent in the nature of the gospel itself, but which actually violate the import of the good news. These limitations we have discussed in previous chapters from several angles of vision — the political, the sociological, the theological, and the ecclesiastical.

The church has limited the good news that God has accepted

the man who accepts God's acceptance (grace) to those who will fit into the structure of grace (the congregation) without too much difficulty. The church has made the mistake of choosing who shall be served by the use of surface phenomena as a criterion: race, class, shave and haircut, and residence in the "right" part of town. All too often the church has been served by men (clerical and lay) who were more concerned to serve themselves than they were to serve God or other (different sorts of) men. The ecology of the average church has been developed in too many instances to parallel the ecology of the white, middle-class suburb — even if the congregation lies in the open country or at the intersection of transportation and commerce in the restless city.

And thus the socially sensitive, the morally aware have turned away in disgust and disquiet from the organization that loudly proclaims itself the body of Christ — yet shows little evidence of bearing his open, joyful, loving, and free Spirit. The hearts of those who sympathize with the poor and the neglected, the ignorant and the hostile, have turned away from that institution which claims to be the servant of man — yet calls continually to be served by men. Against organized religion, then, the radically religious man and woman hurls the often justified charge: You have forgotten that love is greater than faith. You hide from yourself the spiritual diagnosis of James, "Faith without works is dead" (James 2:17).

Karl Barth long ago declared that Ludwig Feuerbach was right — religion is a human work.[8] But while Barth denounced religion and called for faith, the radically religious — the new Christian theologian — calls *for* religion. Loving works are seen as more genuinely the theme and purpose of Jesus' life than formal faith. Therefore, if faith has been shaken in the sensitive, allegiance to love and loving deeds have not.

André Malraux said it for the radical Christian long ago:

" My poor little fellow," he went on at last, " each of us knows only his own unhappiness." His arm pressed Ch'en's.

"Do you think every really religious life is not a daily conversion? . . ."

They were both looking at the sidewalk, and seemed to have
contact only through their interlocked arms. ". . . A daily conversion . . ." the pastor repeated with a weary emphasis, as
though those words were merely the echo of an obsession.
Ch'en did not answer. This man was speaking of himself and
he was telling the truth. Like Ch'en, this man *lived* his idea:
he was something more than a restless bundle of flesh. Under
his left arm, the brief-case and the bomb; under his right arm,
that arm tightly pressing his: ". . . a daily conversion. . . ."
This confidence spoken in a tone of secrecy made the pastor
suddenly appear in a pathetic light. So near to murder, Ch'en
was attuned to every kind of suffering.

"Each night, Ch'en, I shall pray God to deliver you from
pride. (I pray especially at night: it is favorable to prayer.) If
He grants you humility, you will be saved. Now at last I can
read in your eyes and understand, as I could not a while
ago. . . ."

It was with his suffering, and not with his words, that Ch'en
had entered into communion. Those last words, those words of
a fisherman who thinks he feels the pull of a fish, stirred in him
an anger which rose painfully, without altogether banishing a
furtive pity. He was completely baffled by his own feelings.[9]

The radical theologian who believes that he enters into communion with the man Jesus called the Christ is not an atheist
or a nihilist. Indeed, he is the opposite of both, for the tenor
of radical theology is loving optimism, while the bass notes of
its message are calls for solidarity with the suffering ones of
the world. Therefore the emergence of radical Christianity is
not the submergence of the church, but the sign of its reformation; only where the earlier Reformation proclaimed the message of Paul: "The just shall live by faith," the new reformation implores "Love one another" — the message of the man
Jesus. The radical theology proclaimed by Altizer, Hamilton,
van Buren (and others like this writer) is not an antitheology
or an antichurch movement, precisely because it is, at its best,
a call for the reformation of the means by which the message

about Jesus is proclaimed to the world. Nothing could be anti-religious that is concerned with Jesus, nor nihilistic that is optimistic and is committed to the hopeful improvement of the human condition.

But it may be questioned whether the radical theology is not actually a revolutionary or destructive movement instead of a concerned, basically loyal, constructive movement. We judge it to be a reformation or at least the beginnings of a reformation by means of the following definition of reformation: *A reformation is a revolution under the control of an inner, spiritual aim (purpose, goal) instead of being at the mercy of unconscious historical processes.* The radical theology, seen at its best in the early work of William Hamilton, and in the intention of Paul van Buren in *The Secular Meaning of the Gospel,*[10] and in the essays of Altizer and Hamilton in *Radical Theology and the Death of God,* is precisely a spiritual movement designed to recover a sense of the open, loving, and freeing personality of Jesus. It does have an inner spiritual aim, an aim or goal best presented up to this point by Thomas Altizer in *The Gospel of Christian Atheism.* Altizer has written:

Now, what can it mean to seek a radical form of Christian theology or a form of Christian language reflecting and embodying the vision of the modern atheistic Christian prophet? First, it is all too clear that such a language must set itself against the Christian tradition, not simply by way of negating its doctrinal and ritual forms but, rather, by inverting its forms and structures so as to reverse that history revolving about the epiphany of the Christian God. Radical Christians are Protestants insofar as they seek a return to the original Word of faith. But recognizing the reality of the process of history, and the forward movement of Word and Spirit, they are in quest of a renewal of the original Jesus in the spiritual or universal form demanded by the apocalyptic or final age of the Spirit. No radical Christian believes in the possibility of returning to either the word or the person of the original Jesus of Nazareth. Consequently, the radical Christian rejects both the literal and the historical interpretation of the Bible, demanding instead a pneumatic or spiritual understanding of the Word. Above all, the radical Christian seeks a total union with the Word, a union abolishing the priestly, legalistic, and dogmatic norms of the churches, so as to make possible the realization of a total redemption, a redemption actualizing the eschatological promise of Jesus. It is this quest for total redemption — and nothing has so violently aroused the theological spokesmen of the churches — that demands the death of the Christian God, the God who is the sovereign Lord and almighty Creator. The radical Christian must not be thought of as a reformer; he believes that the ecclesiastical tradition has ceased to be Christian, and is now alive only in a demonic and repressive form. No, the radical Christian is a revolutionary, he is given to a total transformation of Christianity, a rebirth of the Christian Word in a new and final form.[11]

Altizer seems to be saying that the radical Christian cannot be considered a reformer in any sense, but must be called a revolutionary. It is just this contention which I am disposed to deny. He goes on to give as his reasons for speaking of a revolution instead of a reformation the following considerations. First, the radical Christian vision demands a thorough rethinking of the meaning of faith and a completely new language in which to express it. Secondly, a radical theology demands that the canon of Scripture be opened again to the possibility that we are living in a new age of the Spirit where the Spirit is revealing himself in completely new ways. Thirdly, the radical Christian must submit himself to the risk of losing all faith.[12] This certainly seems revolutionary. However, the cumulative force of this argument is broken when we consider each element alone. First, almost all creative theologians of the past and present have struggled and are struggling for a new theological language. Again, no creative theologian has ever passed on the Christian tradition without thoroughly rethinking the meaning of faith. If the studies in the contrapuntal tradition reported in my earlier work on radical theology bear any weight at all, then it is clear from them that all the truly contributory members of the Western philosophical and theological community have attempted such a restatement — a restatement that amounts to a complete transformation of faith in some of them, such as Paul, Luther, Kierkegaard, and the nineteenth-century liberal synthesizers who sought to mediate between Christianity and modern culture.[13]

Secondly, it is not the case that the closing of the Biblical canon necessitates a belief that the Spirit cannot reveal himself apart from the Scriptures. Indeed, as Altizer well knows, Catholic theology would be impossible if any such belief were held. Additionally, the study of the history of the development of the canon will show that there are many unresolved problems about just what is and what is not canonical, lying ready to hand for consideration when theology again becomes interested in topics such as these.[14]

Thirdly, Altizer says the radical Christian must take the risk of losing his faith. Nothing could be more traditional than this, for all faith is a risk, as Altizer knows and yet speaks of it as something new because "few theologians have ventured to take upon themselves anything more than a token risk."[15] This is undeniably true, but the fault lies here in the shallow and basically un-Christlike men who have ruled the churches and given position and honor to what I can only call "church theologians," who are long on defenses of the institution and famous for piety but are notoriously lacking in the creativity of mind that allows one to participate in the life of the Spirit that has been let loose in the world since the coming of Jesus.

In summary, all the arguments of Altizer are good, but they are not different in kind from other honest calls for the reformation of the church. Indeed the inner spiritual aim of Altizer's work and the undoubted knowledge that he has of the modern sense of historicity, which precludes his being at the mercy of unconscious historical processes, tend to prove that he is speaking of a reformation rather than a revolution. Despite himself he is a more constructive and helpful theologian than his words about revolution imply.

Altizer in his recent paper on the death of God and Catholic theology has repeated his assertion that we must realize " that it is Christianity itself which must undergo not a reformation but rather a revolution if it is truly to exist and be real in the modern world." [16] This does not change anything, for the import of all his work is to elevate and proclaim the full humanity and the perfect incarnation of deity in Jesus. Indeed, Altizer comes close to orthodoxy, or at least to Tillich and Buber with their speaking of the silence of God, when he says that "we must face the possibility that the ever more pervasive inability of modern man to speak the name of God is a consequence of a movement of God Himself." [17] He also develops some of the consequences of speaking of the church as the body of Christ in such a fruitful way that any theologian taking his suggestions seriously can only contribute to a reformed conception of what being the church really means. Basically, Altizer agrees with the sentiments expressed throughout this book, which hold that the church in the largest sense, as the body of Christ or the true spiritual community, is to " recognize the presence of the Church wherever there is revelation and salvation." [18]

This last insight is straight out of Tillich and is in accordance with much that is basic in the Christian tradition. Again, the emphasis on the identification of the radical Christian with the suffering of Jesus, who perfectly identified himself with the suffering of man, is surely not foreign to a great portion of the Christian tradition. The modern protest that the Christian faith is a flight into unreality, an evasion of suffering and of the responsibility of man for man, which Altizer writes about in *The Gospel of Christian Atheism,*[19] undoubtedly is a widespread misconception of what Christian faith is that is based on the unchristian behavior of many individual "believers" and of many actions on the part of institutional churches. But the practical basis for this protest does not make it a universal truth. The lives of Paul, Francis of Assisi, Ignatius Loyola, Luther, Francis Xavier, Albert Schweitzer, Tom Dooley,[20] and thousands of other dedicated people from the time of Jesus to Mahatma Gandhi [21] to today, belie the impression given — that the identification of the Christian with the suffering of humanity is a dead issue. Indeed, the power of the person of Jesus is seen with the greatest clarity in the life of Albert Schweitzer and in the little man who did not even claim to be a Christian but who, nevertheless, was the most Christlike of men, living in poverty and self-denial for the sake of the outcastes, Gandhi. As Gandhi wrote, Jesus was "a man who was completely innocent, offered himself as a sacrifice for the good of others, including his enemies, and became the ransom of the world. It was a perfect act." [22]

What Altizer has pointed out is the failure of orthodox theology, including neo-orthodox theology, to achieve a faithful rendition of the words and works of Jesus, joined with a truly theological dimension that is possible only when there is a well-developed doctrine of the Spiritual Presence which emphasizes the mystical unity of the follower with that One who is the image of our imitation and also the empowering source of our courage to live as he lived in a radically disoriented world. The answer to the utter drabness and the revolting lukewarmness of the writings of the great number of theologians and the platitudinous proclamations of the organization-tending preachers is not a revolution that says essentially, "Let the church go to hell" and leaves it in its disarray, but rather is a realistic proclaiming of a new order of the Spirit — in short, the preaching of the new reformation.

If modern theology really becomes a functional Christology [23] that speaks of the meaning of Christ on the basis of what he did and what he still does through the Spirit, then we may see a reformation in the church that will produce a morality and theology of full involvement in the needs of the world that will be at once more true to what Jesus is and will also overcome the dichotomy between what we say we believe and what we do. A functional Christology would substitute for

ordinary theology an exhortation that points in two directions
— one toward Jesus as a pattern and example, and the other
toward the neighbor and the needs of man. A functional Christology would be the impetus for Christians to make their
morality and theology the same thing in their lives. It would
have to be based on the full human personality of Jesus' life
and upon his sacred evaluations of the lives of others — of all
others, regardless of mental, physical, moral, economic, or
racial condition. A functional Christology would be indeed a
reduction of the extent and content of Christian theology, and
would need no philosophical basis for itself beyond the everyday more or less scientific, biological basis of modern man's
own estimation of human life as the ultimate value. No other
worlds need be posited, no supernatural order fancifully described, no appeal to faith that flies in the face of reason, but
only an appeal to the intuitive awareness of every human being
that his life is his most precious possession and his first deduc-
tion from this awareness: that the lives of all other creatures
must be similarly precious to them. In this respect a functional
Christology of the type we are suggesting is little different
from Schweitzer's doctrine of "reverence for life," or from
Gandhi's doctrine of Satyagraha, or the "vow of truth."

Such a functional Christology would ask only two questions:
(1) What is more sacred than human personality? and
(2) What is more sacred than living in love that affirms and
preserves our human personality? This may seem like bare
bones instead of a full body for the Christ to the orthodox
mind, but a close reading of the New Testament will reveal
that it includes most, if not all, of the injunctions that Jesus
laid on his disciples — " Love one another as I have loved you,"
" As you wish that men would do to you, do so to them," " Be
kind to one another," and even includes the teachings of Paul,
" Bear one another's burdens, and so fulfil the law of Christ."

Such a functional Christology is really the upshot of Altizer's
criticism and the real content not only of his constructive

efforts but also those of Hamilton, van Buren, and Cox. More than this, such a Christology is close to the primitive Christology of the gospel sans the mythological framework of the first century A.D. which all modern theologians recognize must be either eliminated or reinterpreted so as to make the gospel intelligible to men of our era. Again, such a Christology gives a firm basis for a new reformation of the church because it holds up a concrete and an intensely personal example, Jesus, and includes a highly experiential element within itself as the basis for the reordering of the church's message and mission. Lastly, it removes the artificiality of preaching about abstract doctrines and lays bare the fact that the pulpit should be the place where the message of Christianity meets squarely and honestly the problems and questions of the modern world.

Preaching with a functional Christology as its model must be clearer, more inspirational, more pertinent to human needs than any proclamation based on the recitation of "supernaturally" interpreted events. The picture of the Biblical Jesus, loving and accepting all men and women under all circumstances, has the power to move even modern, secular-minded men quite deeply. The effects of Gandhi's life and work and the proclamation of Martin Luther King's nonviolent approach to civil liberties illustrate this power—although neither man was a complete historical success. Since the earlier radical, Jesus, was also not fully successful, this factor should not be allowed to detract from the positive evaluation we have given the preaching of the human Jesus as the model for a radical Christian life-style in the twentieth century.

Recently there have been a number of articles by established theologians that call for "alternatives to absolutes" in Christian theology.[24] As we would imagine, there have been many other articles and books written that attempt to revive and insist upon the necessity of absolutes, specifically of the supernatural.[25]

The New Image of the Church

It is my belief that if theology is to be possible in the future, it must get off dead center and come to grips with the radical critiques made of the orthodox theological tradition and of the muddling through of the institutional program of the various churches.[26] I have already suggested that the radical critique of Christianity is not something new but is as old as the Western tradition itself and was born out of the same matrix of personalities and events that produced the " orthodox" varieties of Christianity themselves. There have been radically penetrating insights into the shortcomings of those doctrines and practices which have become identified with Christendom throughout its history. One problem with the tradition-centered mind is that it is able to read Kierkegaard and Luther (and others like them) and apparently not recognize the radicality of their message. Altizer, looking at this kind of history-denying myopia feels justified in calling for a revolution, but my assessment of the radical tradition (contrapuntalism)[27] as the most creative and, ultimately, as the most influential element in Christendom, encourages me to believe that a reformation is always possible — now as well as in the past.

We must be very clear that any theological reassessment should be based on the general philosophical outlook of the time in which it is made. In our time that outlook is pragmatic and empirical — definitely not one that gives credence to supernatural claims. Without judging that there is or is not a supernatural order, but simply following the method of the philosophical theologian's craft, we must say that the radically new theology of the new reformation must be based only on the view that recognizes the possibility of the transcendent within *this* world alone. No philosophical basis can be found in modern thought (disregarding the relatively uncritical acceptance of traditional supernaturalism in Neo-Thomism and Protestant fundamentalism, including the efforts of Kenneth Hamilton or the reaction seen in Karl Barth) for any recognition of an order outside or alongside the temporal order or of any world alongside the material universe.

I am convinced that the time to begin the theology of the future is now. For "only the most radical attempts to recover the sense of the sacred and the experience of self-transcendence have any chance of success. A repetition of the Christian positions of the past will do nothing but hinder the possibility that the God of the future might be at least partially known in our time." [28]

By saying that only the most radical attempts to recover the sense of the sacred are meaningful in that they alone have any chance of success, I do not mean to imply that the only avenue along which creative religious thought can proceed is that of the "death of God" theology. Nor do I mean that we must have a revolution that completely overturns all that has been brought into the present from the past through the medium of tradition which has been mediated by the institutional churches and through other structures of Western European culture. I think that revolution is chaotic unless it is a reformatory revolution that is directed by an inner aim that conserves the best elements in the structures which it seeks to change. The answer to the problems raised by the increasing rapidity of social change is not to cast all restraints to the winds and let change run riot. The answer to the problems faced by modern man lies both in an openness to change, which gives him a zest for experimentation, and in a mature resolution to salvage and renew as much of the heritage of the past as is still alive and may possibly be of fundamental importance for the present and the future.

It is this kind of new reformation which I am calling for, and it is this kind of constructive theological work I have desired to point out as the very broad avenue for theology to follow from this point in time. Along this avenue of respect for the past and optimistic zest for the future, combining elements

of the familiar that give a sense of security and the elements
of novelty that are always coming toward us out of the future,
there are individual paths. I do not feel competent, nor do I
think anyone is competent, to say just what those various paths
are or to declare that some of those paths may be closed to
further travel. I only offer my seriously deliberated opinion
that some rather familiar paths are no longer open for useful
travel and some other paths not so familiar are becoming increasingly inviting as roads into a creative and meaningful theological future. I do believe that the path of static orthodoxy
such as is displayed by Kenneth Hamilton, and is actually
made into a caricature by John Warwick Montgomery, is a
path that leads nowhere but to the further decline of respect
for Christendom. On the other hand, I believe the radical openness of Altizer and Hamilton, despite their weaknesses in respect to a more careful handling of the elements within the
tradition, does serve as an exciting point of departure which
should inspire a revival of interest in theology in our time —
and an interest in the genuinely necessary elements of the tradition; e.g., the doctrine of God, Christology, the use of myth
and symbol in religious teaching and liturgy, and certainly not
least (from Altizer's poetic vision), a renewed interest in eschatology. None of these dynamic elements is really made exciting
or even made possible as the subject of serious and sustained
study and popular interest by the warmed-over seventeenth-
century orthodoxy presented by the conservative wing of Protestantism. We might say that we can fix our opinions about
which roads are open and which are closed by Jesus' own criterion of judgment: "You shall know them by their fruits."

From what I have said so far the impression should arise
that I have no new solutions to offer to the problems of the decline in church membership, or to the indifference of many
people to traditional spiritual matters, or to the rank secularity
that is so often condemned on the one side, and on the other
embraced with an ulterior purpose in mind (i.e., to use the

secular to squeeze the sacred back into life) by popular writers and preachers. Indeed, I do not have any solution, other than the obvious one, which I never tire of emphasizing — that the church must recognize its need for reformation. This in itself is no new message, for it is as old as I Peter 4:17: "For the time has come for judgment to begin with the household of God; and if it begins with us, what will be the end of those who do not obey the gospel of God?"

On a more positive note I must observe that the lack of solutions is not really a weakness — while the abundance of many shallow solutions does lead to weakness. Along the way I have spoken of many attempts to change the church or to reform its message, and I have tried to demonstrate that these various attempts are dead ends. Surely knowing that some approaches are unfruitful is at least half the answer to our common problem. Nevertheless I will hazard, in closing, a few guesses into the nature of the new substance and the outlines of the changed image of the church required by our situation in the late twentieth century. The first of these is that the theology of the church of the new reformation must become again catholic in the fullest sense. It must become catholic in the all-embracing way that the theology of Thomas Aquinas was all-embracing — and in the world-affirming way that the theology of Tillich was all-inclusive and open. This catholic theology will be based, if it is to be at all viable, upon a new appreciation of mysticism. This mysticism will be centered on the person of Jesus seen by faith as the Christ. The new theology could find no better starting point for this development than the Christ-mysticism of the apostle Paul.[29] Much has been written in the twentieth century about Paul's Christ-mysticism and one need only suggest that attention be given to the works of Eduard Schweizer,[30] Adolf Deissmann,[31] Albert Schweitzer,[32] John A. T. Robinson,[33] Fritz Neugebauer,[34] Pierre Teilhard de Chardin,[35] Cyril C. Richardson,[36] and Ingo Hermann.[37]

Such a catholic theology based on mysticism will naturally
find itself developing a natural theology. There are many interesting attempts at the formation of a new natural theology
today, some based on the philosophy of Alfred North White-
head, such as that of John B. Cobb, Jr.,[38] and some based on
the fresh approach of Paul Tillich (and on Heidegger), such
as that of John Macquarrie.[39] I rather think that neither of
these approaches will be the most fruitful one in the task of
building a theology for the new reformation. Perhaps the emphasis on following the agenda of the world that I see in the
vision of Altizer will be most helpful — that it is precisely by
living in the midst of the secular world, in the silence of God,
that we shall recover the sense of the sacred. Perhaps, too,
John Cobb will be of help here, for I see in him a reversal of
Tillich's method of correlation in which the questions of man's
existence were raised by philosophy and responded to by theology. Cobb has suggested that natural theology is to ask the
philosophical system it adopts to provide the fundamental vision of reality and the criterion of truth. The Christian tradition is then asked to provide topics and questions to be discussed within the framework of that philosophy.[40] This is close
to the theological method suggested above, i.e., that the discussion of human self-transcendence and the Spiritual Presence must take place within the framework of modern philosophical thought that does not recognize dimensions of reality
alongside or outside the universe as we know and experience
it. Of course, at this point, my suggestion parts company with
John Cobb, who apparently wishes to retain conceptions of the
superhuman within his natural theology.[41]

If there is to be renewal, then there must be repentance on
the part of the leaders of the institutional churches. Renewal
must be repentance in the sense that the church — and for
practical purposes this means its leaders and theologians —
must recognize and turn away from messages and practices
that do not measure up to the radical love seen in Jesus Christ.

Repentance must be a true turning away from the wrong paths of the past and a turning toward more human, sympathetic, and socially active paths in the future. The church's repentance must also be a rejection of all those elements within its message and practice which have separated it from the lower classes on the one side and from the intellectuals and the morally sensitive on the other. The church must also repent of its tendency to self-idolatry. The church can never be the object of the Christian's ultimate concern, nor can it ever be in such a state within time and space that it does not need to be continually reformed. Indeed the very concept of being Protestant demands that the church constantly renew and reform itself in progressive ways. And more importantly, a church cannot be considered Christian if it does not love all men — not abstractly but concretely — reverence all life, and respond to every human need, psychological and physical as well as spiritual, in every nation of the earth. Nothing can be called Christian that exhibits a limited love or a reservation on commitment. It would be desirable for the many ultraorthodox venerators of the Bible to read that Bible someday and discover that in Jesus' theology men and churches were not to be judged by what they believed, or how they phrased their beliefs, or even by the purity of their lives. Rather, as Jesus pointed out in the parable of the Last Judgment (Matt. 25:31-46), we are to be judged by the hungry whom we feed, the thirsty to whom we give drink, the strangers whom we welcome, the naked whom we clothe, the sick whom we visit, and the prisoners whom we comfort. Nothing else is said here by Jesus and nothing else is required of the church but that it do what Jesus did and taught. That is enough. If this can be developed into a Christology like that of "the man for others," if it requires a new ecclesiology, then let it be so, although I do not think it does. And perhaps this basic foundation of the new church can be and must be developed as a theology of social justice. There are indications that this way of procedure may be best. If the new church does take seriously its call to live as Jesus lived, it need follow no other word than: "And what does the LORD require of you but to do justice, and to love kindness, and to walk humbly with your God?" (Micah 6:8).

My conclusion is that the church that does not serve men in their physical, mental, social, and material needs is a false church — a sham, and has nothing to do with Jesus Christ. Anything that the church has taught or done, either as a denomination or as a congregation, that causes men to be idolatrous — to worship the institution, its members or their nation or race, or a doctrine, or the Bible, instead of the perfect human life seen in Jesus — must be rejected. Anything taught by the church that constricts love, that limits fellowship, that excludes (by law or by gentleman's agreements) any race, class, or any other portion of mankind — must be rejected. Anything that would cause men to feel justified in warring on or being suspicious of any portion of mankind or any nation, that would prevent compassion and fellowship from flowing toward certain groups either in peace or in war — must be rejected. Anything that would insulate the church's members from the true face of reality as seen in the suffering of countless men and women in the world, and anything that would seek to enclose the overturning power of love within a shell of indifference or a sense of superiority — must be rejected.

The church of the new reformation must accept the message of the radical thinkers who have proclaimed the death of God as a genuine description of a church that has turned its back on man all too many times. The genius of the new reformers must be one of being Christlike because they are the servants of men as was Jesus. This genius will be found to accord well with the spirit that animated the early disciples and the many reformers and sectarians of Christian history. Like John Wesley, Francis of Assisi, and Paul, they will turn to the poor and to the oppressed and champion them. For them they will have a message that may be inviting. It will be a message proclaimed by those who demonstrate their fidelity by leaving the ninety-nine sheep of the well-to-do classes, who are now all too welcome in the church, to turn to the one lost sheep who lives in a slum or in a depopulated rural area of America, essentially unwanted and despised. Perhaps if such reformers do arise, they may do for that large portion of our population who live below the poverty line, and who are now both the victims of and the malefactors in riots and disorders, what Gandhi did for the *harijan,* the outcastes of India — rebaptize them and reaffirm them as " the children of God."

The new reformation, then, must be a declaration that the people who desire to live as Jesus lived will take part in the forefront of the efforts of mankind to overcome disease, injustice, poverty, discrimination, hatred, criminality, and war. Renewal through such efforts will mean an act of healing, in the sense that the original meaning of salvation meant healing, a growth in integrity and inward self-dignity for the Christian himself, and a drive to make such dignity and inward integrity the property of every man.

Something of the way in which other thinkers are formulating this social direction can be seen in the excellent study *Toward a Theology of Involvement,* by Benjamin A. Reist.[42] We are not concerned here to outline the history of the development of social sensitivity in Protestantism. We are more concerned to emphasize the need for the development of a more theological and profound philosophy of such involvement. This new philosophy of involvement possibly should find its profundity in the simplicity of a functional Christology that discusses the Christ in terms of what he did as well as of what he said and is less concerned with what others, including church councils, have said about his Christhood. In this respect, perhaps such a Christology will develop analogies to what Jesus did by developing the Jesus-like nature of men such as Albert Schweitzer, Gandhi, and Pope John XXIII. By developing a kind of Christology that finds some of its content

in Christlike human personalities, we may be able also to revive interest in the doctrine of the mystical unity of the believer and Christ. The Pauline emphasis on the indwelling of
the Spirit — which is referred to as "the Spirit of Jesus" — lies
ready to hand in Gal. 2:20; II Cor. 3:18; and Gal. 4:6. The
text for such a Christology or pneumatology of human personality could well be Phil. 2:1-2, "So if there is any encouragement in Christ, any incentive of love, any participation in the
Spirit, any affection and sympathy, complete my joy by being
of the same mind, having the same love, being in full accord
and of one mind." This emphasis upon Spirit-bearing personalities is of course directly related to the deepest wellsprings
of piety and belief throughout Christian history, although it
has been more often seen in the sectarian than in the sophisticated church member. Such a development must follow if
there is to be any theological content and any inspirational
power behind the obvious change in the mission (that is, of
the church's conception of its mission) of Christendom from
the "saving" of individual souls "out of" the world to the effort to humanize man by revealing his possibilities, social and
spiritual, to him, and by helping him to achieve the full development of his potentialities — both as an individual atom
in the social mass and through the creation of freer social
structures.

In this mission of healing and fulfilling, there will be no
other resources but the Gospel picture of Jesus as the Christ or
of Jesus as the man for others, in the terms of our day. But
through the serious desire to participate in the style of life
seen in Jesus, we can expect to increase in inner integrity and
in the power to carry the picture of Jesus through word and
through action to mankind as a whole.

Notes

Notes

I. Is the Antithesis of Christianity " Christendom "?

1. Gabriel Vahanian, *The Death of God: The Culture of Our Post-Christian Era* (George Braziller, Inc., 1961).

2. Paul Tillich, *The Protestant Era,* tr. by James L. Adams (The University of Chicago Press, 1948).

3. William Hamilton, *The New Essence of Christianity* (Association Press, 1961).

4. Thomas J. J. Altizer, *Oriental Mysticism and Biblical Eschatology* (The Westminster Press, 1961).

5. Hamilton, *The New Essence of Christianity,* pp. 35 ff.

6. This writer was one of those invited to the Conference on Radical Theology held at the University of Michigan, Ann Arbor, on October 26–29, 1966. I also attended the Conference on America and the Future of Theology held at Emory University, Atlanta, Georgia, on November 18–20, 1965. The papers produced by the latter conference have been published in the volume *America and the Future of Theology,* edited by William A. Beardslee (The Westminster Press, 1967). Hamilton has abjured his position in *The New Essence of Christianity* in his article " The Death of God Theologies Today "; in *Radical Theology and the Death of God,* by Thomas J. J. Altizer and William Hamilton (The Bobbs-Merrill Company, Inc., 1966), pp. 23–50. Also see " The New Optimism — from Prufrock to Ringo," *The New Essence of Christianity,* pp. 157–169.

7. Altizer, *Oriental Mysticism and Biblical Eschatology,* p. 199.

8. See John C. Cooper, *The Roots of the Radical Theology* (The Westminster Press, 1967).

9. *Ibid.*

10. *Ibid.*, pp. 15 ff.

11. Friedrich Nietzsche, *The Philosophy of Nietzsche* (Modern Library, Inc., 1954), pp. 951 ff.

12. Cooper, *The Roots of the Radical Theology*, pp. 71–93.

13. John A. T. Robinson, *Honest to God* (The Westminster Press, 1963), and *Christian Morals Today* (The Westminster Press, 1964); also David L. Edwards, *The Honest to God Debate* (The Westminster Press, 1963).

14. Joseph Fletcher, *Situation Ethics: The New Morality* (The Westminster Press, 1966).

15. Cooper, *The Roots of the Radical Theology*, pp. 84–93.

16. Paul Tillich, *Systematic Theology*, Vol. III (The University of Chicago Press, 1963), p. 165.

17. *Ibid.*

18. Thomas J. J. Altizer, *The Gospel of Christian Atheism* (The Westminster Press, 1966), p. 23. Cf. Cooper, *The Roots of the Radical Theology*, pp. 140–152.

19. I am not unaware of the works of H. Richard Niebuhr and Reinhold Niebuhr on these same topics — I refer here not to the knowledge of sociodynamic facts but to sociologically derived doctrinal " substance." Most religious thinkers are aware of the historically conditioned nature of particular churches, Tillich is speaking of the identification of the point of transcendence with ideals derived from such " conditionedness." Vahanian, *op. cit.*, speaks clearly of this phenomenon.

20. Tillich, *Systematic Theology*, Vol. III, p. 167.

21. James Pike, " Tax Organized Religion," *Playboy*, Vol. 14, No. 4 (April, 1967), pp. 93, 100, 144–148.

22. Tillich, *Systematic Theology*, Vol. III, p. 169.

II.   *The Problem of Change: Reformation or Revolution?*

1. For the works of George Burman Foster, see: *The Finality of Christian Religion*, 2d ed. (The University of Chicago Press, 1909); *The Function of Religion in Man's Struggle for Existence* (The University of Chicago Press, 1909); *The Function of Death in Man's*

Struggle for Existence, ed. by T. G. Soares (The University of Chicago Press, 1915); *Christianity in Its Modern Expression,* ed. by D. C. MacIntosh (The Macmillan Company, 1921); *Friedrich Nietzsche,* ed. by Curtis Reese and A. E. Haydon (The Macmillan Company, 1931). For the works of Harry Emerson Fosdick, see: *Adventurous Religion and Other Essays* (Harper & Brothers, 1926); *As I See Religion* (Harper & Brothers, 1932); *Christianity and Progress* (Fleming H. Revell Company, 1922); *The Greatness of God* (London: William Collins Sons & Co., Ltd., 1961); *The Hope of the World* (Harper & Brothers, 1933); *The Meaning of Faith* (Association Press, 1917); *The Meaning of Prayer* (Association Press, 1917); *The Meaning of Service* (Association Press, 1921); *Modern Use of the Bible* (The Macmillan Company, 1924); *The Power to See It Through* (Harper & Brothers, 1935); *Spiritual Values and Eternal Life* (Harper & Brothers, 1927); *What Is Vital in Religion* (Harper & Brothers, 1955).

For an interesting study of the earliest American " radical theologian," George B. Foster, see C. H. Arnold's article, " The Death of God — 1906," in *Foundations, A Journal of Baptist History and Thought,* Winter, 1968 (Rochester, N.Y.).

2. " Evangelical Springtime " (" Pen-ultimate"), copyright 1967 Christian Century Foundation. Reprinted by permission from the April 26, 1967 issue of *The Christian Century,* p. 575. " Pen-ultimate " quotes from the University of Minnesota's *Minnesota Daily* of February 14, 1967.

3. Cooper, *The Roots of the Radical Theology,* pp. 94 ff.

4. Bob Dylan, *Highway 61 Revisited* (CL 2389 Record; Columbia Record Company, 1965).

5. Hamilton, " The New Optimism — from Prufrock to Ringo," *The New Essence of Christianity,* pp. 157–169.

6. John C. Cooper, " Ultra-Conservatives and Lutherans Today," *The Lutheran Quarterly,* Vol. XVIII, No. 3 (August, 1966), pp. 214–226.

7. Edward Carnell, quoted in *Handbook of Christian Theology,* ed. by Marvin Halverson (Meridian Books, Inc., 1958), p. 142.

8. Charles Harvey Arnold, " Against the Furious Men," *Frontiers,* Vol. XVII (January, 1966), pp. 8–18.

9. Vahanian, *The Death of God,* pp. 14 ff.

10. Arnold, *loc. cit.*, pp. 11–12.

11. Eric Hoffer, *The Ordeal of Change* (Harper Torchbooks, Harper & Row, Publishers, Inc., 1966).

III.   *The Point of Institutional Concern*

1. Will Herberg, *Protestant, Catholic, Jew* (Anchor Books, Doubleday & Company, Inc., 1960).

2. Donald E. Boles, *The Bible, Religion and the Public Schools* (Collier Books, The Macmillan Company, rev. ed., 1963).

3. Joseph Gaer and Ben Siegel, *The Puritan Heritage: America's Roots in the Bible* (Mentor Books, New American Library of World Literature, Inc., 1964), p. v.

4. *Ibid.*, p. 13.

5. Peter L. Berger (ed.), *The Human Shape of Work* (The Macmillan Company, 1964). See Ch. 6, pp. 211–241.

6. Max Weber, *The Protestant Ethic and the Spirit of Capitalism*, tr. by Talcott Parsons (Charles Scribner's Sons, 1958).

7. Edward A. Feaver, " The Death of Religion and the Rebirth of the Church," *Skandalon 2* (Student Interracial Ministry), Winter, 1967.

8. Victor Obenhaus, *The Church and Faith in Mid-America* (The Westminster Press, 1963).

9. H. Richard Niebuhr, *The Social Sources of Denominationalism* (first publ. in 1929, Meridian Books, Inc., 1962), p. 6.

10. *Ibid.*, pp. 17–21.

11. *Ibid., passim.*

12. *Ibid.*, p. 38.

13. David W. Barry, " The Fellowship of Class," *Cities and Churches*, ed. by Robert Lee (The Westminster Press, 1967), pp. 274 ff.

14. *Ibid.*, p. 274.

15. Obenhaus, *op. cit.*, p. 120.

16. *Ibid.*

17. Herberg, *op. cit.*, pp. 65–66; *Yearbook of American Churches,* 1967 (Department of Publication Services, National Council of the Churches of Christ in the U.S.A.), p. 213.

18. Herberg, *op. cit.*, pp. 65–66.

19. *Yearbook of American Churches,* 1967, p. 220.

20. Herberg, *op. cit.*, pp. 65–66.

21. The differences between the figure of 62.2 percent of the general population who *claim* to be Protestant, and the percentage of actual Protestant Church members in relation to the total population should be well understood. In 1960, 35.4 percent of the general population was actually listed on Protestant Church rolls. In 1965, this figure was 35.6 percent. Information from *Yearbook of American Churches*, 1967, p. 219.

22. Herberg, *op. cit.*, p. 3.

23. Obenhaus, *op. cit.*, p. 160.

24. *Yearbook of American Churches*, 1967, p. 196. Total number of all religious bodies and sects reported to *Yearbook*, 1967, was 251. In 1936, the last year a U.S. Census included this category, there were 256 bodies reported in the United States. This was before the incorporation of Alaska and Hawaii as states.

25. Publication of the National Lutheran Council, A *Mighty Fortress*, Vol. XVII, No. 4 (August, 1967), p. 3.

26. *Ibid.*

27. *U.S. Bureau of the Census, 1957 Census of Governments*, Vol. 1, No. 1, p. 1. Also see John C. Cooper, *The Christian and Politics* (Board of Parish Education, Lutheran Church in America, 1968), pp. 68 ff.

28. Jesse Lemisch, *Towards a Democratic History* (Radical Education Project Occasional Paper; Students for a Democratic Society), p. 1.

29. W. W. Sweet, *The Story of Religion in America* (Harper & Brothers, 1950). See also Abdel Ross Wentz, *A Basic History of Lutheranism in America* (Muhlenberg Press, 1955); Chapters 19 and 20 discuss the disruption of the various Lutheran bodies during the Civil War.

30. See C. L. Bachman, *John Bachman, Letters and Memories of His Life* (Charleston: Walker, Evans & Cogswell Co., 1888); also see Lemisch, *op. cit.*, p. 1. For many insights into the Lutheran attitude toward Negroes and slavery before the Civil War, and during it, see Douglas C. Strange, " Slavery and Salvation " in *Lutheran Forum*, Vol. I, No. 9 (September, 1967), pp. 4–7. John Bachman, although he befriended many Negroes, was deeply prejudiced against them. He felt they were inherently inferior and wrote, " The

European race is, in form and color, as much of an improved race as the African is a degenerate one " (Bachman, *The Doctrine of the Unity of the Human Race Examined on the Principles of Science;* Charleston, S.C., 1850), p. 237.

31. Kenneth Scott Latourette, *A History of Christianity* (Harper & Brothers, 1953), p. 1261.

32. Feaver, *loc. cit.,* pp. 4–5.

33. C. N. Parkinson, *Parkinson's Law* (Ballantine Books, Inc., 1957). Parkinson's Law is a humorous observation on the natural capacity of men to waste time. It says, " Work expands so as to fill the time available for its completion."

34. James Pike, "Tax Organized Religion," *Playboy,* Vol. 14, No. 4 (April, 1967), pp. 93, 100, 144–148.

35. Donald L. Metz, *New Congregations: Security and Mission in Conflict* (The Westminster Press, 1967), p. 15.

36. *Ibid.,* pp. 79–80.

37. *Ibid.,* Ch. 8, pp. 117–133.

IV.   A Theological Look at the Church

1. See the works of Altizer and Hamilton, *Radical Theology and the Death of God;* William A. Beardslee (ed.), *America and the Future of Theology* (The Westminster Press, 1967); Henlee H. Barnette, *The New Theology and Morality* (The Westminster Press, 1967); Fletcher, *Situation Ethics: The New Morality;* Hamilton, *The New Essence of Christianity;* Lotte and Werner Pelz, *True Deceivers* (The Westminster Press, 1966); John A. T. Robinson, *The New Reformation?* (The Westminster Press, 1966), *Christian Morals Today, Honest to God;* Richard L. Rubenstein, *After Auschwitz* (The Bobbs-Merrill Company, Inc., 1966); Vahanian, *The Death of God;* and Paul M. van Buren, *The Secular Meaning of the Gospel* (The Macmillan Company, 1963).

2. Gordon Rupp, *The Old Reformation and the New* (Fortress Press, 1967), pp. 49–57.

3. The materials in this section are based on Paul Tillich, *Systematic Theology,* Vol. III, Part IV, pp. 111–296 (herein cited as S.T.) (The University of Chicago Press, 1963); and John C. Cooper, "The Significance of the Pauline Spirit-Christology for the Doctrine of the Spiritual Presence in the Theology of Paul Tillich,"

unpublished Ph.D. dissertation, the University of Chicago, 1966.

4. See Joseph Haroutunian, *God with Us* (The Westminster Press, 1965), and Herbert W. Richardson, *Towards an American Theology* (Harper & Row, Publishers, Inc., 1967), pp. 141 ff.

5. Haroutunian, *op. cit.*, pp. 73–83.

6. Martin Luther; see Regin Prenter, *Spiritus Creator,* tr. by John M. Jensen (Muhlenberg Press, 1953).

7. Tillich, *S.T.*, pp. 111 ff.

8. *Ibid.*, p. 111.

9. Tillich, *The Protestant Era.*

10. *Ibid.*, pp. 94–112, " Nature and Sacrament."

11. Karl Jaspers, *Way to Wisdom* (Yale University Press, 1954), pp. 82 f.

12. Tillich, *S.T.*, p. 139.

13. *Ibid.*, p. 140.

14. *Ibid.*, p. 149.

15. *Ibid.*

16. *Ibid.*, pp. 149–150.

17. *Ibid.*, pp. 150–152.

18. *Ibid.*, Acts 2:1-11.

19. *Ibid.*, p. 151.

20. *Ibid.*

21. *Ibid.*

22. *Ibid.*, p. 152.

23. *Ibid.*

24. In this connection, Tillich's discussion in *S.T.*, pp. 245–249, is especially important.

25. *Ibid.*, pp. 152–153.

26. *Ibid.*, p. 155. The Pauline references are to I Cor. 12:12-31; Gal. 2:20.

27. *Ibid.*, pp. 157–158; also Tillich, *The Protestant Era.*

28. Tillich, *S.T.*, pp. 182 ff.

29. *Ibid.*, pp. 182–188.

30. *Ibid.*, pp. 184–185.

V. *The New Reformation of the Twentieth Century*

1. Paul Tillich, *The Protestant Era,* tr. by James L. Adams, abr. ed. (The University of Chicago Press, 1957).

2. Vahanian, *The Death of God.*

3. Robinson, *The New Reformation?*

4. Paul M. van Buren, *The Secular Meaning of the Gospel.*

5. Harvey Cox, *The Secular City* (The Macmillan Company, 1965). Also see Gibson Winter, *The Suburban Captivity of the Churches* (Collier Books, The Macmillan Company, 1962).

6. Thomas J. J. Altizer, *Mircea Eliade and the Dialectic of the Sacred* (The Westminster Press, 1963).

7. Altizer and Hamilton, *Radical Theology and the Death of God.*

8. Paul Tillich, *The Future of Religions,* ed. by Jerald C. Brauer (Harper & Row, Publishers, Inc., 1966).

9. Dietrich Bonhoeffer, *Prisoner for God: Letters and Papers from Prison* (The Macmillan Company, 1954).

10. James Pike, "Tax Organized Religion," *Playboy,* Vol. 14, No. 4 (April, 1967), pp. 93, 100, 144–148.

11. The underground church is largely made up of those people who remain church members while active in civil rights, the peace movement, etc.

12. Robinson, *The New Reformation?* p. 13.

13. *Ibid.,* p. 34.

14. The authoritative church confessional documents of the churches springing from Luther's and Melanchthon's direct involvement in the old Reformation are recorded in *The Book of Concord,* Eng. trans. (Concordia Publishing House, 1952). Lutherans have always (and many still do) taken these documents (the Augsburg Confession, the Apology, etc.) seriously. The definition of the church is given in the Augsburg Confession, Arts. VII–VIII.

15. On Menno Simons, see George H. Williams, *The Radical Reformation* (The Westminster Press, 1962), pp. 387 ff.

16. Martin Luther, "Against the Robbing and Murdering Hordes of Peasants," *The Works of Martin Luther,* Vol. IV (A. J. Holman Company and Castle Press, 1931), pp. 248–254.

17. See Gottfried G. Krodel, "Erasmus — Theologian," in *The Cresset,* Vol. XXX, No. 10 (October, 1967), pp. 11–15. Krodel reports on the great progress made in Erasmus studies in Germany since 1962.

18. Friedrich Schleiermacher, *On Religion: Speeches to Its Cul-*

tured Despisers, tr. by John Oman (Harper Torchbooks, Harper & Brothers, 1958).

19. Cooper, *The Roots of the Radical Theology,* see Ch. IV, pp. 95–114.

20. *Ibid.,* pp. 62 ff.

21. Thomas J. J. Altizer, " Catholic Theology and the Death of God," in *Cross Currents,* July, 1967.

22. Samuel Beckett, *Waiting for Godot* (Grove Press, Inc., 1954).

23. André Malraux, *Man's Fate,* tr. by Haakon M. Chevalier (Modern Library, Inc., 1961), p. 220. Copyright, 1934, by Harrison Smith and Robert Haas, Inc.; renewed, 1961, by Random House, Inc. Quotations used by permission of Random House, Inc.

24. " All of Us or None," Bertolt Brecht, *Selected Poems,* tr. by H. R. Hays (Grove Press, Inc., 1959), pp. 103–105. Used by permission of Harcourt, Brace & World, Inc.

VI. *The Form of the Church of the New Reformation*

1. Cooper, *The Roots of the Radical Theology,* pp. 15 ff.

2. On psychedelic drugs, see H. A. Abramson (ed.), *The Use of LSD in Psychotherapy* (Josiah Macy, Jr., Foundation Publications, 1960). Also see Warren R. Young and Joseph R. Hixson, *LSD on the Campus* (Dell Publishing Company, Inc., 1966).

3. Mao Tse-tung, *Quotations from Chairman Mao-Tse-Tung* (Foreign Languages Press, 1966), and Mao Tse-tung, *Mao Tse-tung: Anthology of His Writings,* ed. by Anne Fremantle (Mentor Books, New American Library of World Literature, Inc., 1962).

4. See Jack Newfield, *A Prophetic Minority* (New American Library, Inc., 1966), esp. pp. 13–24.

5. On the " death of God " theology, see Cooper, *The Roots of the Radical Theology;* Altizer and Hamilton, *Radical Theology and the Death of God;* Altizer, *The Gospel of Christian Atheism.*

6. Rubenstein, *After Auschwitz,* and " Judaism and the Death of God," *Playboy,* Vol. 14, No. 7 (July, 1967), pp. 69 ff.

7. Thomas J. J. Altizer, " Catholic Theology and the Death of God," *Cross Currents,* July, 1967, p. 4. Also see Cooper, " The Significance of the Pauline Spirit-Christology on the Doctrine of the Spiritual Presence in the Theology of Paul Tillich."

8. Introduction by Karl Barth in Ludwig Feuerbach, *The Essence of Christianity* (Harper Torchbooks, Harper & Brothers, 1957), pp. x ff.

9. Malraux, *Man's Fate*, pp. 177–178.

10. Van Buren, *The Secular Meaning of the Gospel*. For Hamilton, see *The New Essence of Christianity*.

11. Altizer, *The Gospel of Christian Atheism*, pp. 25–26.

12. *Ibid.*, pp. 26–27.

13. Cooper, *The Roots of the Radical Theology*, pp. 71–93.

14. See B. F. Westcott, *A General Survey of the History of the Canon of the New Testament*, 7th ed. (The Macmillan Company, 1896).

15. Altizer, *The Gospel of Christian Atheism*, p. 28.

16. Altizer, *loc. cit.*, p. 1.

17. *Ibid.*, p. 10.

18. *Ibid.*, p. 6.

19. Altizer, *The Gospel of Christian Atheism*, p. 21.

20. See Tom Dooley, *The Edge of Tomorrow* (Mentor Books, New American Library of World Literature, Inc., 1962); *The Night They Burned the Mountain* (Mentor Books, New American Library of World Literature, Inc., 1962); and *Deliver Us from Evil* (Mentor Books, New American Library of World Literature, Inc., 1962).

21. See Thomas Merton (ed.), *Gandhi on Non-Violence* (New Directions, 1965). Also see Louis Fischer, *Gandhi: His Life and Message for the World* (Mentor Books, New American Library of World Literature, Inc., 1962). For an American adaptation of Gandhi's active Christlike love, see Martin Luther King, Jr., *Strength to Love* (Pocket Books, Inc., 1964).

22. Merton (ed.), *op. cit.*, p. 34.

23. See John McIntyre, *The Shape of Christology* (The Westminster Press, 1966). McIntyre asks: "Whence do [Christological] models derive? The answer that commends itself to my judgment is that the creation of models is part of the function which imagination fulfils in theological activity. Theology has been singularly slow to allow imagination a place within its sacred precincts; and one ought not to be surprised if as a result a good deal of theology has been correspondingly unimaginative" (p. 173). This is most certainly a true saying!

24. Bernard E. Meland, "Alternatives to Absolutes," *Religion in Life*, Vol. 34 (1965), pp. 343–351. Also see T. R. Miles, "On Excluding the Supernatural," *Religious Studies*, Vol. 1, No. 2 (1966), pp. 141–150; Alastair McKinnon, "Unfalsifiability and Religious Belief," *Canadian Journal of Theology*, Vol. 12, No. 2 (1966), pp. 118–125; and Edith F. Hunter, "Where Liberal and Neo-Orthodox Meet," *Religion in Life*, Vol. 34 (1965), pp. 398–405. Also compare Kenneth Hamilton, "Verifiable Christianity: From Arnold to van Buren," *Canadian Journal of Theology*, Vol. 11 (1965), pp. 156–163.

25. Kenneth Hamilton, *loc. cit.*, and also see *The System and the Gospel* (The Macmillan Company, 1963); John Warwick Montgomery, "The Theologians' Craft: A Discussion of Theory Formation and Theory Testing in Theology," *Concordia Theological Monthly*, Vol. 37 (1966), pp. 67–98. Also see Robert W. Jenson's interesting book *A Religion Against Itself* (John Knox Press, 1967).

26. Cooper, *The Roots of the Radical Theology*, pp. 156–157.

27. *Ibid.*, pp. 15–49.

28. *Ibid.*, p. 157.

29. See Cooper, "The Significance of the Pauline Spirit-Christology on the Doctrine of the Spiritual Presence in the Theology of Paul Tillich," Ch. I, pp. 4–85.

30. Eduard Schweizer, "Spirit of God," *Bible Key Words*, ed. by G. Kittel, Vol. III (London: Adam & Charles Black, Ltd., 1960).

31. Adolf Deissmann, *Paul — A Study in Social and Religious History*, tr. by W. E. Wilson (first publ. 1921; Harper & Brothers, 1957).

32. Albert Schweitzer, *The Mysticism of Paul the Apostle* (London: Adam & Charles Black, Ltd., 1953), and *Paul and His Interpreters*, tr. by W. Montgomery (London: Adam & Charles Black, Ltd., 1948).

33. J. A. T. Robinson, "The Most Primitive Christology of All?" *Journal of Theological Studies*, New Series, Vol. VII (1956), and *The Body — A Study in Pauline Theology* (SCM Press, Ltd., 1957).

34. Fritz Neugebauer, *In Christus: En Christoi* (Vandenhoeck & Ruprecht, 1961).

35. Pierre Teilhard de Chardin, *The Divine Milieu* (Harper Torchbooks, Harper & Row, Publishers, Inc., 1965).

164 RADICAL CHRISTIANITY AND ITS SOURCES

36. Cyril C. Richardson, "Discussion: The Tri-Unity of God," *Union Seminary Quarterly Review*, Vol. XXI, No. 2, Part 2 (January, 1966).

37. Ingo Hermann, *Kyrios und Pneuma. Studien zur Christologie der paulinischen Hauptbriefe* (Studien zum Alten und Neuen Testament, Band 2) (Kösel-Verlag, 1961).

38. John B. Cobb, Jr., *A Christian Natural Theology* (The Westminster Press, 1965).

39. John Macquarrie, *Principles of Christian Theology* (Charles Scribner's Sons, 1966).

40. Cobb, *op. cit.*, p. 265.

41. See John Cobb, "Christian Natural Theology and Christian Existence," *The Christian Century*, March 3, 1965, p. 265.

42. Benjamin A. Reist, *Toward a Theology of Involvement* (The Westminster Press, 1966). This study of the thought of Ernst Troeltsch may be fruitfully compared with Philip Hefner's *Faith and the Vitalities of History* (Harper & Row, Publishers, Inc., 1966), a study of the work of Albrecht Ritschl.

Index

Index